The
Witches Qabala

The Witches' Qabala

The Pagan Path
and the Tree of Life

Ellen Cannon Reed

WEISER BOOKS
Boston, MA/York Beach, ME

First published in 1997 by
Red Wheel/Weiser, LLC
York Beach, ME
With offices at
368 Congress Street
Boston, MA 02210
www.redwheelweiser.com

Library of Congress Cataloging-in-Publication Data

Reed, Ellen Cannon.
  The witches Qabalah: the pagan path and the tree of life/
Ellen Cannon Reed. — Rev. ed.
    p. cm.
  Includes bibliographical references and index.
  ISBN 0-87728-880-1 (v.1 : pbk. : alk. paper)
  1. Cabalah. 2. Neopaganism. I. Title.
BF1611.R43   1997
135'.47—dc21   97-9197
                                                        CIP

TCP
Typeset in 11 point Galliard
Printed in Canada

08 07 06 05 04 03 02
10 9 8 7 6 5 4

The paper used in this publication meets the minimum requirements of
the American National Standard for Information Sciences—
Permanence of Paper for Printed Library Materials Z39.48-
1992(R1997).

To Margo, who gave me the torch to carry, and to Christopher, best friend and aim-crier.

CONTENTS

LIST OF ILLUSTRATIONS

INTRODUCTION TO
THE SECOND EDITION

THE GODDESS AND THE TREE was first completed in 1983. As I write this, we are a few months away from 1997 and I've been given a wonderful opportunity by Weiser: the chance to add what I've learned in the last 13 years to what I'd written before, and to change what I'd written to reflect the changes I've undergone. I had material to add even between the completion of the book and its original publication.

This is not to imply that the original edition was faulty, but that life and further study have added to that which I wish to share with you. Very little has been changed, but much has been added, and some things have been rewritten because I've found more effective ways to express my ideas.

When I started working on this new edition, I made shameless use of my friends. Not only did I pick their brains about what should be added, but if they gave me actual material they had used, I included it. (That'll teach 'em.)

If you found the earlier edition of this book useful, I believe you'll find the new one even more so. A great deal of the credit for this goes to those friends mentioned above, to students in our coven, and to others who have shared with me.

PREFACE

MY COVEN TRAINING contained the usual subjects—ritual, herbology, the seasons, astrology, spell-casting and Qabala. It wasn't until much later, however, that I discovered Qabala was not only an unusual subject in Craft training, but was shunned by many as an unsuitable subject for any pagan tradition. The subject was my favorite, and what I considered my most valuable tool was a no-no for my fellow pagans. Why?

I started rereading my books on Qabala and discovered why: All these books were written by ceremonial magicians or Christian Qabalists who not only didn't write for pagans, but worded their books in such a way as to alienate those with beliefs similar to mine. It was probably not deliberate, but that was the result. I was not alienated because I was so involved in my subject that I passed right over such passages. Someone new to Qabala and unsure of the subject, on the other hand, might be easily offended.

It also seemed that some of the authors went out of their ways to present the material in an obscure manner. Of course, a struggle to understand can make the final understanding greater, but I don't believe that was the intent. Whether it was carelessness or style, I don't know, but the result was to keep people from understanding.

Pagans were missing the value of Qabala because of the way the information was worded, and that seemed a horrible waste to me.

I presented a lecture on Qabala for Pagans and the reaction of the audience confirmed my belief that Qabala was acceptable to pagans if presented correctly. I am attempting such a presentation here.

As I write, I am trying to imagine who you, my readers, are. My imagination presents me with the following groups:

—students of the occult (Craft and Qabala) who are studying
with a teacher;

—solitary students who do not have a teacher, either by choice
or from lack of opportunity;

—Qabalists who are either wondering what business a witch has
writing about Qabala and are horrified at the whole idea, or
are delighted to see the Qabala made available to more people;

—teachers, group leaders, High Priests and High Priestesses,
etc. of pagan groups (covens, groves, etc.), seekers who have
not yet found their path;

—all the rest of you.

To the last group—Blessed be!

To the penultimate group, I will you success in your
search, for the finding of your proper path is a singularly joyful discovery. The Craft is a lovely path, though not for everyone. If you find, as you read, that you relate to the ideas
reflected here, are drawn to a path that reveres life and recognizes both Lord and Lady, I suggest you read *The Truth
About Witchcraft Today* and *Wicca: A Guide for the Solitary*
by Scott Cunningham, *Wicca: An Old Religion for a New Age*
by Vivianne Crowley, and *A Witch Alone* by Marion Greene.
Whatever your way may be, there is material here that can be
of use to you.

To the first group—students with a teacher, I don't believe
there is anything here which could interfere with what you are
being taught, but it would be courteous to discuss it with your
teacher. Better yet, lend them this book and then discuss it.

To the solitaries by choice: Greetings, and I hope you find
this work useful.

To the other solitaries: Good luck in finding a teacher.
Methods of doing so are included here.

To the teachers: In my own experience as High Priestess,
I've found Qabala an invaluable help. With it, you can guide
your students toward direct spiritual experience, understand,
and provide help for and even predict specific problems. You
can also use the Qabala to contact specific energies for your rit-

uals. All this is in addition to the help it can provide in your own spiritual work.

To my fellow Qabalists who are in favor of my work: Thank you for your support, and Blessed be!

To the Qabalist who is about to strike me with lightning: My, what an intolerant, narrow attitude you have! If ancient Qabalists had had your attitude, the study would never have grown past the original glyph. The Tree of Life holds all of Creation and more. Surely there is room for different points of view.

I tried to keep all of you in mind as I wrote, although the book is aimed at paganfolk. I have not attempted to write a definitive book on Qabala. In a lifetime or two I might, but not here, not now. What I have tried to do is create a bridge to the Qabala, to introduce you to the subject in such a way that you will see its value and be able to pursue its study without being alienated.

There is plenty to work with in this book alone, but I hope you'll study further, seek out the recommended books. If you are intrigued enough to do that, I will be content. If you go even further and decide to make Qabala part of your spiritual work and/or include it in the studies of your group, I will be delighted.

THE CHARGE OF THE GODDESS

Listen to the words of the Great Mother, who was of old called amongst men, Isis, Artemis, Astarte, Dione, Melusine, Aphrodite, Diana, Arionrhod, and by many other names.

Whenever you have need of anything, once in the month and better it be when the Moon is full or new, then shall you assemble in some secret place and adore the spirit of Me, Queen of all Witcheries. There shall you assemble, who have not yet won my deepest secrets and are fain to learn all sorceries. To these shall I teach that which is as yet unknown. You shall be free from all slavery, and as a sign that you be free, you shall be naked in your rites. You shall sing, feast, make music and love, all in my presence, for mine is the ecstasy of the spirit, and mine is also joy upon Earth. My law is love unto all beings. Mine is the Secret that opens upon the door of youth, and mine is the cup of the wine of life, the cauldron of Cerridwen, which is the Holy Grail of Immortality. I am the Gracious Goddess who gives the gift of youth unto the heart of mankind. I give knowledge of the Spirit Eternal, and beyond death, I give peace and freedom and reunion with those who have gone before. Nor do I demand aught of sacrifice, for behold, I am the Mother of all things and my love is poured out upon the Earth.

Hear you the words of the Star Goddess, She, in the dust of whose feet are the hosts of heaven, whose body encircles the universe.

I am the beauty of the Green Earth, and the White Moon among the stars, and the mystery of the Waters. I call unto your soul: Arise and come unto me. For I am the Soul of Nature who gives life to the universe: from me all things proceed and unto me all things return. Beloved of all the Gods and men, let my worship be in the heart. Rejoice, for behold, all acts of love and pleasure are my rituals. Therefore, let there be beauty and strength, power and compassion, honor and humility, mirth and reverence within you. And you who think to seek me, know that your seeking and yearning will avail you not, unless you know the Mystery, that if that which you seek you find not within yourself, you will never find it without. For behold, I have been with you from the beginning, and I am that which is attained at the end of desire.

(from the traditional charge)

I seek the Crown
of Wisdom and Understanding
That Might and Mercy
In balance bring Beauty,
Victory and Glory
Find their Foundation
In the Kingdom.

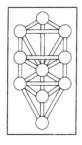

THE MYSTERIES
OF THE WEST

All things began in order.
— Sir Thomas Browne[1]

BEGINNING IN THE LATE 19th century, a great interest
in the Eastern philosophies was born in the West. In the days
preceding and during a tremendous growth in scientific
knowledge, in industry and in later years a reach for outer
space, many developed an interest in their "inner space" and
yearned for something not provided by the religions they had
inherited.

Psychology and psychiatry had begun their exploration of
the human mind, and even members of that august fraternity,
most notably Carl Gustav Jung, realized that the conscious
mind was only a small part of a true inner self, in spite of the in-
clination of the scientific community to accept only that which
could be proven "scientifically."

The Eastern philosophies did offer an understanding of
that self—a contact with it—and many people found comfort
and a measure of peace in what was offered. Madame Blavatsky
and her fellow Theosophists were among the first to introduce
these ideas (albeit somewhat mixed with various Western ideologies) to the West. In the 1960's, this interest experienced a
rebirth, spurred by its adoption by many well-known figures.

---

[1] Sir Thomas Browne, *The Garden of Cyrus,* chapter 5. *The Oxford Dictionary of Quotations* (London: Oxford University Press, 1985), p. 95.

However, as so many discovered, the differences between the East and West are numerous. Not the least of these is a vast difference in attitude and culture. East and West do not share the same mind-set; the Oriental philosophy of withdrawal from life is not practical in a world where that withdrawal must contend with the hurry-scurry, make-a-living, do-it-now atmosphere of Western society. The West needed something different: a *Western* esoteric philosophy, suitable to *its* way of life.

Such a philosophy, in fact several of them, have existed for many years, some since before the Christian era. Those of us who have found our way to the Craft of the Wise Ones (Witchcraft or Wicca) and other similar beliefs know this; we live one of them. Our path is one which reveres a Heavenly Mother as well as a Heavenly Father, cherishes all that lives, accepts Divinity within ourselves as well as without, and embraces a belief in reincarnation.

There are others, and we are fortunate to live in an age when information on all the magical paths is so easily available. We are no longer restricted to the knowledge inherited and developed by our own small groups; we are in contact with other traditions; we learn and share and grow. Techniques, tools, methods, and knowledge from others have added to modern life and spirituality. One such source is the Qabala.

The obvious question for one new to the Qabala is, of course, "What is it?" Those authors most respected in this strange and mysterious subject all describe it differently. W. G. Gray calls it "symbolic representation of the relationship believed to exist between the most abstract Divinity and the most concrete humanity."[2] He also calls it "a family tree linking God and man together with angels and other beings as a complete conscious creation."[3] Dion Fortune defines Qabala as "an attempt to reduce to diagrammatic form every force and factor in the manifested universe and the soul of man; to correlate them

[2] W. G. Gray, *Ladder of Lights* (York Beach, ME: Samuel Weiser, 1993), p. 11.
[3] W. G. Gray, *Ladder of Lights*, p. 11.

to one another and reveal them spread out as on a map so that the relative positions of each unit can be seen and the relations between them traced . . . a compendium of science, psychology, philosophy, and theology."[4]

Israel Regardie puts it more simply: "The Qabala is a trustworthy guide, leading to a comprehension both of the Universe and one's own Self."[5] Gareth Knight defines it as "a system of relationships among mystical systems which can be used . . . to open up access to the hidden reaches of the mind."[6] It has been called a framework, a stepladder for spiritual growth, and a tool for the study of comparative religion. A. LaDage calls it a system "for obtaining direct religious experience," while W. E. Butler describes it as "*a method of using the mind* in a practical and constantly widening consideration of the nature of the universe and the soul of man."[7]

The Qabala is all of these, and more. My own favorite definition, which paraphrases Dr. Regardie, is "a file cabinet to contain the Universe." That may sound frivolous, but it is not; nor is it inaccurate. The Qabala provides a filing cabinet for the mind, giving you a place for everything. Even better, the Qabala offers you a retrieval system, not only for information *you* have placed in this cabinet, but eventually for information placed there over the centuries by other practitioners of Qabalism. The Qabala is a way of tying all your studies together and relating them to each other, enabling you to understand each more completely.

It is also a tool that can be used to guide your personal growth, and to measure it. It can be used for personal and for group work, by solitary, student and teacher. And, while it is not effective after only a quick glance at the material, it is not at

---

[4] Dion Fortune, *The Mystical Qabalah* (York Beach, ME: Samuel Weiser, 1984), p. 13.

[5] Israel Regardie, *Garden of Pomegranates* (St. Paul, MN: Llewellyn, 1970), p. i.

[6] Gareth Knight, *Practical Guide to Qabalistic Symbolism* (York Beach, ME: Samuel Weiser, 1978), p. 7.

[7] A. LaDage, *Occult Psychology* (St. Paul, MN: Llewellyn, 1987), p. 9; and W. E. Butler, *Magic and the Qabala* (London: Aquarian Press, 1964), p. 22.

all difficult to use. In the following chapters, you will find information that can be put to use immediately.

How can a philosophy attributed to a patriarchal, monotheistic religion possibly relate to a polytheistic, matriarchal religion? Not only does the Qabala relate well to paganism, but the mystical Qabala relates better, in my opinion, to the beliefs of paganism than it does to modern Judaism. Qabala recognizes the feminine in Deity (in other words, the Goddess) as a vital part of the energies of the Universe. Because of this recognition, Qabala was proclaimed heresy by orthodox Judaism at one point in history, and even today is not well thought of by many Jews. This recognition of the Goddess is the first point in favor of the Qabala, as our spiritual ancestors discovered long ago.

At present, I'm told that Qabala is not taught to anyone under the age of 35 unless they are married. The age limit could reflect a desire for maturity in students, but I'm at a loss to understand how being married can qualify you. Perhaps modern Hebrew teachers have found something a lot racier than I have in this subject.

The word *qabala* comes from a Hebrew word *QBL* (Qoph Beth Lamed), "to receive." In ancient Hebrew, there were no written vowels until approximately 700 A.D., so when transliterated to our alphabet, an "a" was written in as the nearest sound. This transliteration accounts for the varied spellings of the word: Kabbalah, Qabalah, etc. You are free to choose the spelling you prefer.

Legend has it that Qabala was given to ancient Hebrew scholars by an archangel for the purpose of helping them to experience the Mysteries, and to allow them to help others to experience them. (I deliberately did not say "teach the Mysteries," for, by definition, Mysteries are those "received" teachings which cannot be taught.) According to the same legend, only the glyph known as the Tree of Life and only one correspondence for the Names of Power were given to the ancients. All other correspondences have been added since.

Another version of the legend holds that the Qabala was given to Moses on Sinai at the same time he was given the Ten Commandments. Moses passed this knowledge on to Joshua, who passed it on to the Judges, who passed it on as they saw fit. If the Qabala did come from (or through) Moses, it is worthwhile to consider his upbringing. Moses was raised as an Egyptian prince, and probably trained as a priest in the Egyptian Mysteries. It is therefore possible that much of that training and those mysteries were incorporated into the Qabala.

It matters not. It does not even matter if, as some skeptics contend, the Qabala was pieced together by Moses de Leon in the 12th century. The Qabala is valid; it works. That is what is truly important. Moreover, it works today, in our world, in our culture, in our way of life, in our religion. It is a living system, a growing one, ancient yet ever new.

During the first centuries after Christ, when the early Christian Church was growing in power, the Jewish religion was considered as pagan as any other pre-Christian religion, and they all went underground together. No doubt there was a great deal of sharing and interchange between members of these faiths, and it is very probable that, at this time, non-Hebrew scholars became aware of the Qabala, recognized its value, and blithely appropriated it for their own use. My teacher once told me, "A good witch is eclectic. She'll steal anything that works." In the search for spiritual understanding, this is a common occurrence, and rightly so.

The Qabala began to develop in a new way. We added planetary attributions, the tarot, gods and goddesses, jewels, animals, elements, plants, and a multitude of other correspondences to the Tree. These additions have taken place over the centuries, and are still taking place today. It is of this expanded Qabala that I speak—the magical or mystical Qabala.

The Tree has grown and flowered since its introduction to humanity. It has been filled with ideas, with spiritual experiences, with the efforts and hearts of hundreds of thousands of those who have studied and used it. All of this is there for your use and your benefit. You can learn from it and in time, make your own contribution to it. The study of the Qabala, the adoption of it into your life and your thoughts, puts you in touch with knowledge placed there by those who have gone before, your elder brethren, through their own adoption and use of this magical, mystical tool.

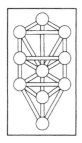

2

THE TREE OF LIFE

Thou cunning'st pattern of excelling nature . . .
—Shakespeare[1]

THE FIRST AND LARGEST step in showing you the value of the Qabala is to explain some of the significance of the glyph known as the Tree of Life (see figure 1, page 8). As shown on the diagram, the glyph consists of ten spheres, joined by 22 "paths." These spheres, *sephiroth* in Hebrew, are arranged in three triangles with the tenth sphere hanging below the other nine. They have both Hebrew and English names (figure 2, page 9), as well as various alternative titles which express their meaning, their being. The spheres and the paths that join them are like "file drawers" of the universal filing cabinet described earlier. If you prefer a computer analogy, you can think of the spheres and paths as the directories on your hard drive.

The study of Qabala involves, among other things, the study of the meanings of these spheres, and their relationship to one another. One aspect of this study is the arrangement of the spheres into "pillars," the spheres on the left of the Tree being in one pillar, those in the center in another, and those on the right in a third (see figure 3, page 10).

Traditionally, these pillars are called (from left to right) the Feminine Pillar, the Middle Pillar, and the Masculine Pillar, or the Pillar of Severity, the Pillar of Mildness or Equilibrium, and

---

[1] William Shakespeare, Othello, Act V, i, l 34.

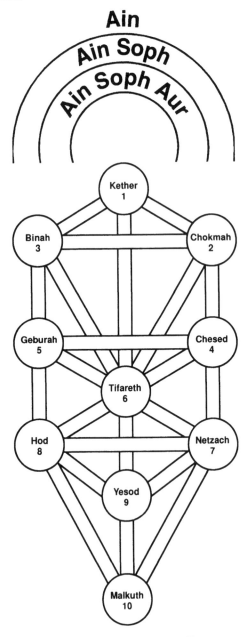

Figure 1.   The Tree of Life.

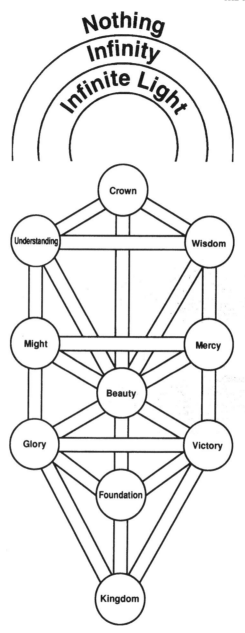

Figure 2.   The Tree of Life with English Names.

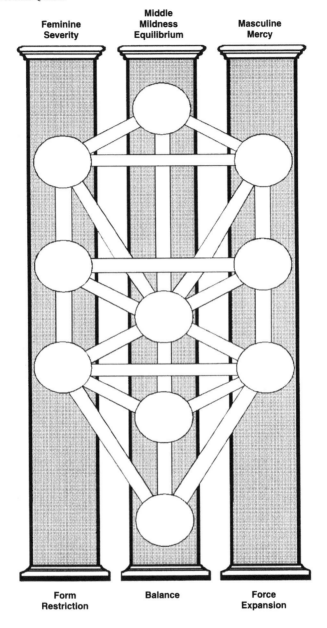

Feminine
Severity

Middle
Mildness
Equilibrium

Masculine
Mercy

Form
Restriction

Balance

Force
Expansion

Figure 3.   The Pillars.

the Pillar of Mercy. Both sets of titles are appropriate, but limited. I use two other sets of titles which are more inclusive:

The Pillar of FORM	The Pillar of BALANCE	The Pillar of FORCE
The Pillar of RESTRICTION		The Pillar of EXPANSION

The reasons for these attributions will become clear as we study the individual spheres. In a playful mood, I once attributed the AD&D (a popular role-playing game) alignments to the Pillars: Lawful, Neutral, and Chaotic.[2]

CORRESPONDENCES ON THE TREE OF LIFE

Each sphere has various correspondences—file folders for the file drawers, or files in your directories. These correspondences have been related to the spheres for various reasons, some obvious, some obscure. Half the fun and part of the learning process lies in trying to understand why this or that was attributed here or there. Each authority differs slightly in these attributions, though many are fairly standard. I have chosen those that work best for me. Remember that these are not "carved in stone." If others occur to you, by all means add them. If, after study, you prefer others, those are correct for you.

While some of these correspondences may relate to each other, quite often they do not. All the file folders in your "A," drawer have names that begin with "A," but that could be all they have in common. It is a serious mistake to assume that one correspondence equals another. One correspondence may put you in tune with one aspect of the sphere, while another may touch quite another aspect.

---

[2] Playful? Yes, it is not only possible to approach Qabala in a playful mood, but a darned good way to learn.

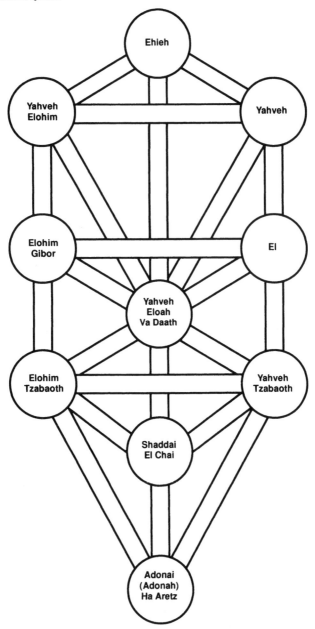

Figure 4.   Names of Power.

Each sphere has a Name of Power, also known as a Deity name, and these present one of the first stumbling blocks for pagans (see figure 4, p. 12). These names were developed, after all, by a patriarchal culture, and most of them are masculine. However, the Names refer to the ultimate, the Unknowable, which is neither sex or both, in its different aspects, so in spite of their literal translations, they have no sex in themselves. There is a reason for not simply doing away with them. An attempt has been made to provide alternate translations which express the aspect represented, but that is not really necessary. Simply consider the Names as those "barbarous names of evocation" we are so often accused of using. They are nothing more or less than sounds, vibratory rates which, whatever their literal meaning, can be used to tune you in to the wavelength of the sphere in question. Their translation is not important. Their effect in use is.

Perhaps the most useful correspondence, one that you can use from the very start, is the Magical Image—a picture designed to represent the sphere and the energy it signifies (figure 5, page 14). Like so many magical things, these images have been used by so many, so often, and with such concentration that they have developed a power of their own. They work both ways: Meditation on a sphere can bring an image to mind, even if you do not know what the Magical Image should be, and meditation on an Image can put you in contact with the energies of the sphere they represent.

If you're interested in performing an experiment, after you have finished this chapter, spend some time meditating on the following: A young queen, crowned and throned. Make notes on the ideas that come to you.

As you may be beginning to see, this is not just a two-dimensional diagram. The Tree of Life is a living tree. It can be used to experience and understand the universe, from deep inside you to the farthest reaches of the most abstract divinity.

Each sphere has a planetary attribution, sometimes called its "mundane chakra" (figure 6, page 15). A planetary attribution is an astrological figure whose significance will help those

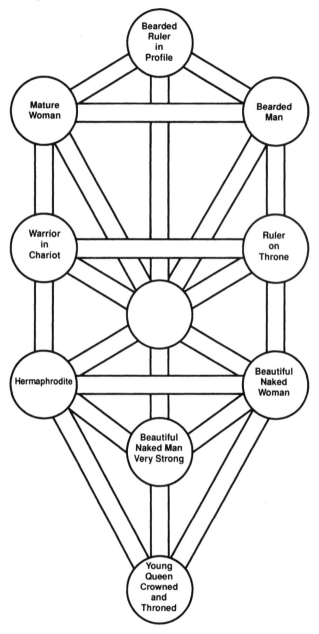

Figure 5. Magical Images.

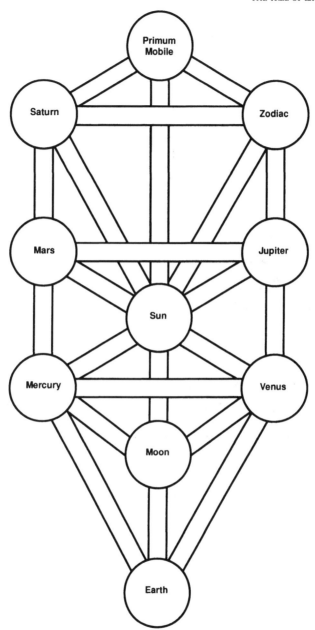

Figure 6.   Planetary Attributions.

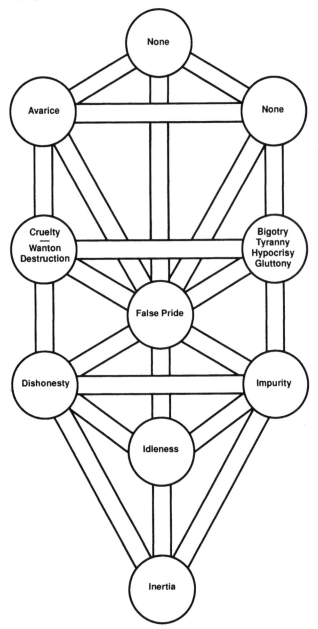

Figure 7.   Vices of Each Sphere.

with an astrological background to understand further the sphere to which it is attributed, or, conversely, to help those without an astrological background to understand further the significance of the planet. The powers represented by these astrological figures constitute one of the "Four Worlds" of the Qabala (see chapter 13).

For most spheres, there is also a Vice and a Virtue which represent the reactions to the energy of a sphere as it begins to have an effect on a human being. Humans being imperfect vehicles (at this stage of development), the negative reaction, or Vice, usually manifests itself first (see figure 7, page 16). Ideally, this will purify into the positive reaction, or Virtue (see figure 8, page 18). The Vice and Virtues are also indications of the amount of a particular kind of energy present. The right amount of energy will manifest as a positive aspect or Virtue; an imbalance or overflow of energy as a negative aspect, or Vice. Dion Fortune describes a sphere's Virtue as the result of spiritual initiation into that particular sphere.

In addition, each sphere has a Pagan Mythology attached to it: deities and mythological figures that correspond to that sphere (figure 9, page 19). This is one of the ways in which Qabala can be used in the study of comparative religion. If we know that Ptah can be attributed to a specific sphere, and that Brahma is attributed to the same sphere, we understand both a little better. Various deities are attributed to more than one sphere, depending on different aspects of that deity.

The deities I know best are the Ancient Egyptian ones, and so I often use those as examples. Other authors may make other attributions. None of these differences imply that one is right and the other wrong. In all pantheons, deities are multi-faceted and can appear in several spheres. You may disagree entirely with my attributions. Good! It proves you are thinking!

Perhaps the most important correspondence of each sphere is its spiritual experience, usually called "A Vision of . . ." something or other (figure 10, page 20). The term "vision" is a bit misleading. These are not blinding flashes of gods and goddesses appearing before you, no "St. Paul on the road to

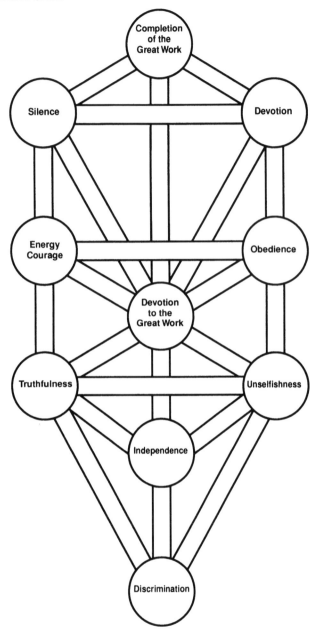

Figure 8.   Virtues of Each Sphere.

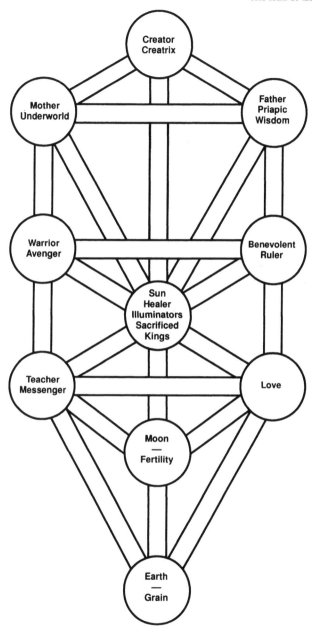

Figure 9.   Deities on the Tree.

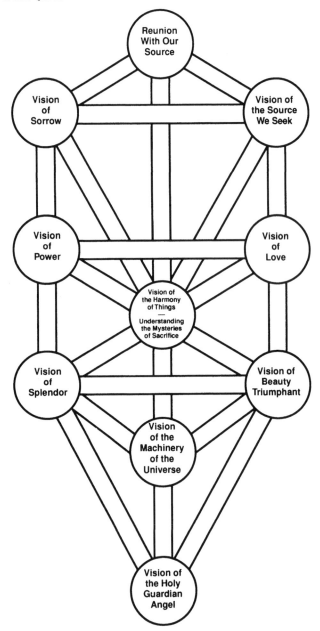

Figure 10.   Spiritual Experiences of the Spheres.

Damascus" experiences. They are types of understanding, of awareness. The realization that you *have* this awareness can come in a blinding flash, but the awareness has been growing and developing within you, day by day, slowly, until you become aware of your awareness. You know that you know, and that you *have* known for some time.

These experiences, so meaningful, so important, so glorious, are also a source of frustration, because they cannot be shared. You can't give them to others. You can talk for hours and hours, and it will not help others to understand if they haven't had the experience—and no words are necessary if they have. These are the Mysteries, those things which cannot be taught, the "received teachings" which must be experienced to be learned.

If I say, "The Universe is a safe place. You cannot truly be harmed. And there is a plan, a pattern to it all. Things are as they should be. I know that to be true. I know it for a certainty," there are those who will agree, will understand, will nod. To them I say, "Have you ever tried to convince others?" It can't be done, unless they have had the experience known as "The Vision of the Machinery of the Universe." If they have, there is no need to convince them; they know.

Here is one of the areas where Qabala is a blessing to teachers. You cannot *teach* this awareness, but, by using the Qabala, you can guide students toward it. Within the Qabala, you'll find material for meditations, exercises, rituals that will not only lead students toward specific spiritual experiences, but also will help them with other specific problems, mundane or spiritual.

Perfume, (or incense) is assigned to each sephira (figure 11, page 22). This can be used to accompany meditation or ritual work to help you even further to tune in to the proper energy. That's what working with the Qabala is: tuning your mind to a specific wavelength. The Tree of Life shows you where the "station" is, and you use meditation or ritual to tune in.

Various precious and semi-precious stones, animals, plants, etc. are also attributed to each of the sephiroth (figures 12 and 13, pages 23 and 24). Like the perfumes, these can be used to

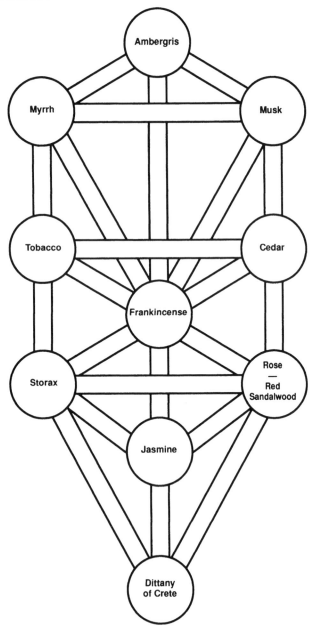

Figure 11.   Perfumes and Incense on the Tree.

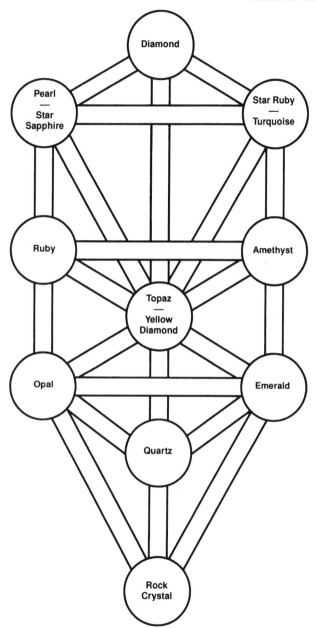

Figure 12.   Stones on the Tree.

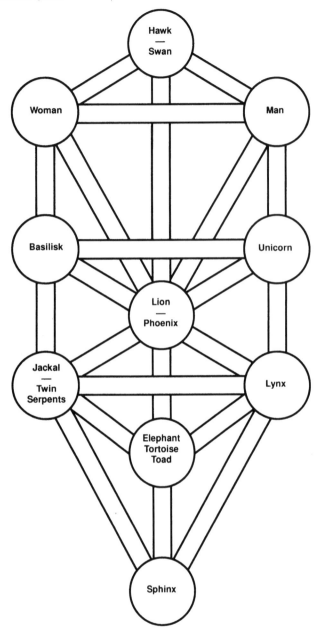

Figure 13.   Animals on the Tree.

add effect to magical workings. In addition, each sphere has four colors attributed to it, one for each of the Four Worlds of the Qabala. These worlds are discussed briefly in another chapter (figure 14, page 26).

There is an archangel assigned to each sephira, as well as a "choir" of angels. Do not, however, confuse the angels and archangels of the Qabala with the winged angelic images you may be used to. Angels are beings (or forms of energy) created for special and precise purposes. They are capable of their own specialties—"divine robots," so to speak (figures 15 and 16, pages 27 and 28).

Archangels are more versatile than angels. They are the "supervisors," if you will, although that is a very simplistic way to describe such mighty and holy beings.

Angels and archangels are more highly evolved than humans, but, unlike humans, they are at the peak of their evolution. They will always be as they are. Humankind, however, will one day surpass them and rejoin our source, the God and Goddess. We are currently in the situation of the college student who will one day be Dean of the College. Whatever our future status, while we are students, we have to listen to our teachers.

Angels and archangels are sexless, though I usually use the masculine pronoun when referring to one of the archangels. It seems more polite than "it." You might find it interesting, though, that members of our coven came to see one of the archangels as female. We each did so individually, without knowing for a long time that the others were seeing the same thing. (English names for the angel choirs are provided in figure 17 on page 29.)

In this new edition, I've included three correspondences gleaned from Colin Low's excellent book, *Notes on Kaballah*, for some of the spheres. The first of these is the Briatic Correspondence—a quality which gives you an idea of the way the sephira expresses itself. The next, the Illusion, "characterizes the way in which the energy of the sphere clouds one's judgement." The third, the Obligation, is, again, according to Low,

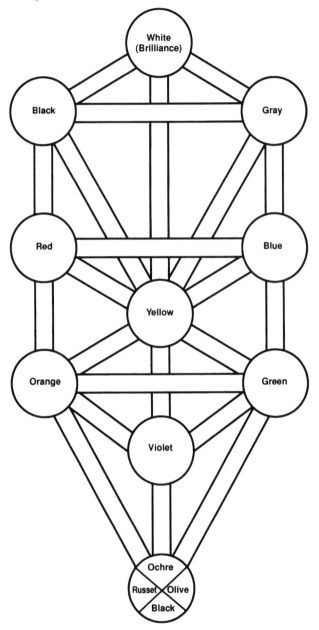

Figure 14.   Colors on the Tree.

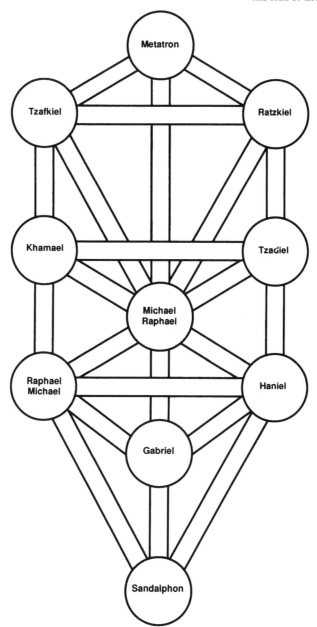

Figure 15.   Archangels on the Tree.

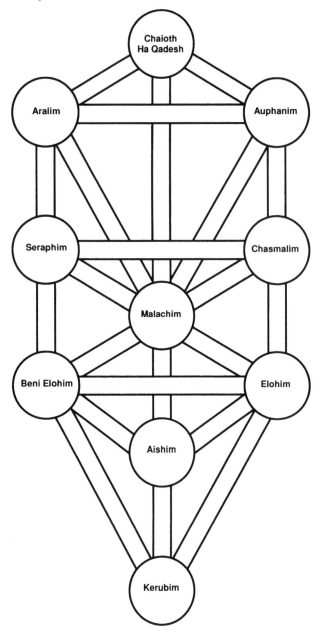

Figure 16.   Angels (Hebrew).

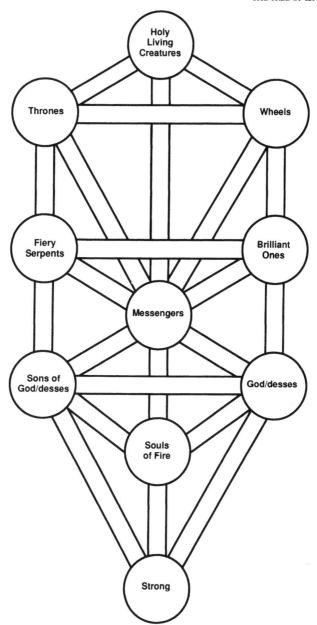

Figure 17.   Angels (English).

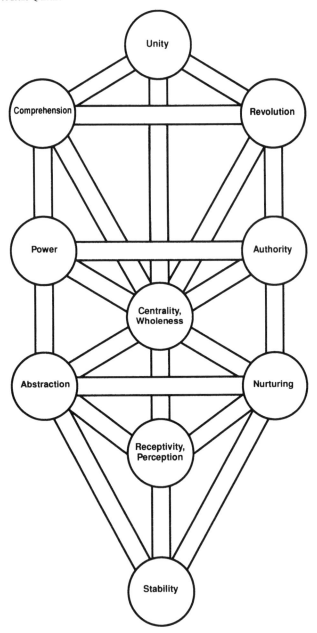

Figure 18.   Briatic Correspondences.

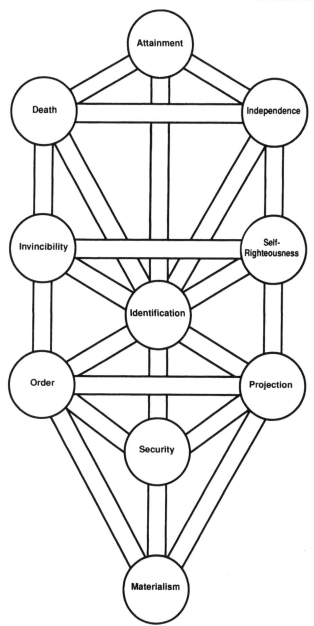

Figure 19. Illusions of Each Sphere.

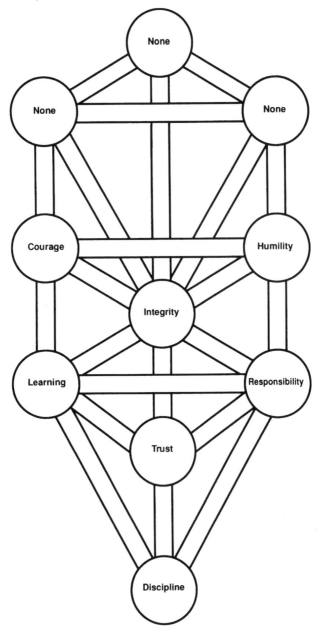

Figure 20.   Obligations of Each Sphere.

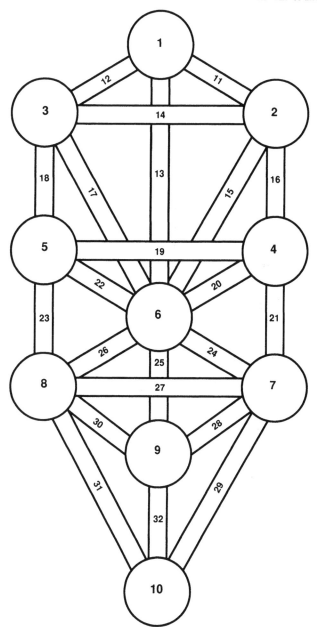

Figure 21.   The Paths on the Tree.

"a personal quality which is demanded of the Initiate at this level."[3] (See figures 18, 19, 20 on pages 30, 31, 32.)

I've used these exactly as I've used the writings of other authors. I've considered them, meditated, played with the ideas, and so forth. The result may or may not resemble Low's original ideas.

Many of these attributions will make perfect sense to you at first reading. Others will not. Don't worry if you don't comprehend everything at once. Someday when you're puttering around, everything will come together in your mind and you will have what is known as a "mystical *Aha!* experience." You'll understand.

As described above, there are twenty-two paths connecting the spheres of the Tree of Life (figure 21, page 33). Think of these paths as states of becoming, while the spheres are states of being. The study of the paths is an interesting one, but I will not delve too deeply into that study in this book. A few paths will be discussed briefly in chapter 14.

THE TREE OF EVIL

There is also a "Tree of Evil" said to be below the Tree of Life. This may well be a later and unnecessary addition to the Qabala. I don't feel it has a place in Craft beliefs, so you'll find no "evil" energies in this book, although the energies represented by the spheres of the Tree can be used in ways which can bring harm to others. It is possible to learn some control of these powers without the spiritual development that should accompany that knowledge. It's stupid, but it's possible.

It is *not* possible to harm others without ultimately bringing harm to ourselves, for we are all one, and what we do to others we are doing to ourselves. To harm ourselves, even indirectly, is stupid at the very least. Ideally, the person who could commit such an act is to be pitied. Perhaps souls in a more ad-

---

[3] Colin Low, *Notes on Kaballah.* See author's material on the web: http://www. digital-brilliance.com/kab/nok/index.html. No page numbers are available.

THE TREE OF LIFE   35

vanced state than mine can actually feel that pity. Those who do harm will learn, painfully, and their lessons will be all the more painful for the harm they have inflicted.

Have you ever looked back on a small cruelty you committed as a child and regretted it? Children are not deliberately cruel, but they do not understand that other children are "real." Empathy and sympathy come with maturity. Black magic is only done by those who do not understand that other people are part of themselves, that "what's going out is what's coming in."

It is very easy to say, and almost as easy to accept, that we should sympathize with those who commit harmful acts. Yet it is very difficult to do. Nevertheless, it is what we should do. If you remember what you felt when you recalled your childhood cruelties—how much greater will be the anguish they feel when those who practice black magic realize what they've done.

TEMURA, GEMATRIA, AND NOTARICON

There are other aspects in the study of the Qabala that I will not deal with in this book. These, *temura, gematria,* and *notaricon,* are methods of searching for hidden meanings, especially in the Old Testament.

Temura is related to modern cryptography. The addition, subtraction, and substitution of letters in words, and the reading of words in different orders are among its methods.

Notaricon has many modern practitioners. It deals with acronyms—taking the first (and sometimes last) letters of words in a sentence and creating a word which signifies the whole sentence. Two modern examples of notaricon are "laser" (Light Amplification by the Stimulated Emission of Radiation) and "radar" (Radio Detecting And Ranging).

Gematria is the numerology of the Qabala. Each letter in the Hebrew alphabet also represents a number. Gematrists believe words that have the same "number" have the same meaning, or represent the same essence.

If these aspects of the Qabala interest you, you can find more information on them in other books, some of which are listed in the bibliography.

Let us move on to a study of the individual spheres and how they may be useful to you.

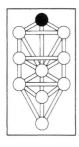

3

I AM THAT WHICH IS ATTAINED AT THE END OF DESIRE

Nature that fram'd us of four elements,
Warring within our breasts for regiment,
Doth teach us all to have aspiring minds:
Our souls, whose faculties can comprehend
The wondrous Architecture of the world:
And measure every wand'ring planet's course,
Still climbing after knowledge infinite,
And always moving as the restless Spheres,
Will us to wear ourselves and never rest,
Until we reach the ripest fruit of all,
That perfect bliss and sole felicity,
The sweet fruition of an earthly crown.
—Christopher Marlowe[1]

TO TAKE THE FIRST STEP in understanding the meaning of the Tree, look at figure 2 (page 9) which shows the Tree with its English names. As you can see, there are three veils of "negative existence," which precede the first sphere, the Ain, the Ain Soph, and the Ain Soph Aur: "Nothing," "Infinity," and "Infinite Light." These veils are, and they are not; they precede being as we can comprehend it. That which is our source is a concentration of these states of pre-being. The first state of being is the first sphere, Kether, whose color is "brilliance." When painting

---

[1] Christopher Marlowe, *Conquests of Tamburlaine*, Part I, 1 869, in *The Oxford Dictionary of Quotations*, 2nd ed. (London: Oxford University Press, 1941), p. 309.

the Tree, use the brightest white that you can find, but see it as the brightest imaginable swirling, moving light. Kether means the "crown" and is placed above the head, so is it just beyond your comprehension.

Kether is called "Primum Mobile," the "first mover," the "first swirlings." It is not manifestation. It is the cause of manifestation, the first idea of being. Kether is what Richard Bach calls "The Is."[2] Before Kether there *is* nothing. Kether is before force, before form, before the idea of force and form. It is the idea of a computer, or the idea of a hard drive.

When dealing with the human mind, all analogies with the Ultimate must be inadequate, but I offer this one for your consideration and contemplation. Imagine you are standing in the dark some distance away from a large wall, aiming a flashlight at that wall. At first, the light won't even touch the wall. As you move closer, the tiniest bit of light will reach the wall—so little that it seems a lessening of darkness rather than an addition of light. Move forward slowly. Soon there will be a faint circle of light, and as you move even closer, that circle will become more distinct, smaller, brighter, more concentrated. Eventually you will see a smaller dot of even brighter light in the center of that large circle. That's Kether, coming together out of the Ain Soph, that which is before being. One of Kether's symbols is a point within a circle.

The Deity Name, the Name of Power is EHIEH, "I Am." This name gives another hint toward the understanding of Kether, for it can be compared to a breath. Whisper it to yourself, inhaling on the "Eh" sound and exhaling on "he-yeh." That breath, that exhalation, signifies the primal force of Kether becoming the next sphere, Chokmah.

The Archangel of Kether is Metatron, giver of the Qabala. The Angels are the "Holy Living Creatures," usually depicted as a man, an eagle, a lion, and an ox (bull). The astrologers among

---

[2] Richard Bach, *Illusions: The Adventure of a Reluctant Messiah* (New York: Dell, 1981), p. 47.

you will recognize these as the symbols for the fixed signs of the zodiac. The angels symbolized, however, are as far removed from the zodiacal signs as the zodiac signs are from the physical manifestations.

The deities usually attributed to Kether are the Creator/Creatrix gods and goddesses: Gaea, Cronos, Ptah, Brahma, etc., depending on your own idea of creation. If you believe in a primordial ocean, Kether is that ocean, or the Cosmic Egg, or the time before the Big Bang, or the cause of the Big Bang.

A planetary attribution for Kether is difficult. Meditation on the First Swirlings or empty space about to become less empty may be helpful to you.

The Magical Image of Kether is an "ancient bearded ruler seen in profile." Here we encounter another "chauvinistic" attribution. We must remember the society that produced the Qabala, in which a beard denoted age and wisdom. They combined that age, the beard, and the concept of rulership to form an image which embodied that which was beyond knowing, the source of all wisdom. The key phrase here is "seen in profile." The significance of the figure is that only one side is seen; the other is out of sight and will remain so until we rejoin our source, become one with our beginnings.

Kether is androgynous, both male and female, both God and Goddess. Therefore, it would not be inappropriate for pagans to imagine, when using this image, that the side unseen is feminine—the Goddess. Kether is feminine, receptive to the Ain Soph, and the Unseen Goddess signifies a concentration of the not-being of the Ain Soph into the idea of being, which is Kether.

The Spiritual Experience of Kether is "Union with God," or "Reunion with the Source." This is the culmination of the Great Work, the goal for which we all strive, on our own path, in our own way, aware or unaware. Obviously this is not an experience we have while incarnate. If we did, we wouldn't be.

Kether's virtue reflects its Spiritual Experience. It is Attainment, completion of the Great Work. Kether has no vice.

The Briatic Correspondence of Kether is expressed as Unity, of course; becoming one with the beginnings, the source, with all of creation.

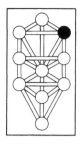

4

I HAVE BEEN WITH THEE FROM THE BEGINNING

To know that what is impenetrable to us really exists,
manifesting itself as the highest wisdom and the most ra-
diant beauty, which our dull faculties can comprehend
only in the most primitive forms—this knowledge, this
feeling, is at the center of true religiousness. In this sense,
and in this sense only, I belong to the ranks of the de-
voutly religious men.

—Albert Einstein[1]

AS MANY QABALASTIC TEXTS SAY, "Kether overflows
into the next sphere," Chokmah, whose name means "Wisdom." In Chokmah, pure being becomes pure force—not physical force, however, as this sphere is still a long way from
physical manifestation. Chokmah is the *idea* of force, spiritual
force. Chokmah is the Ultimate Positive, the God.

This sphere and those directly below it are said to be on
the Masculine Pillar, and Chokmah sits at its head. Chokmah is
the Great Stimulator, dynamic thrust, the Great Fertilizer. Its
Name of Power is JHVH, Yahveh or Yah, meaning "Lord." I
sometimes translate this as "Father of all."

Many sources use the name *Jehovah* for *JHVH*, but this is
incorrect. Ancient Hebrew, when written, recorded only con-
sonants. In Judaism, the word represented by *JHVH* is not
spoken except in prayer and in a worship service. The word

---

[1]Albert Einstein, *What I Believe* in *The World Treasury of Religious Quota-*
tions (New York: Hawthorne Books, 1966), p. 847.

Adonai is spoken whenever the letters *JHVH* are written. In the 12th century, a copyist was apparently translating Hebrew script into the Roman alphabet, and was confused by the vowels written under the word *JHVH*, as a reminder to the reader to say "Adonai." Thus appeared the word *Jehovah.* The proper word is probably *Yahveh* or *Yah.*

Names of Power are usually vibrated in use, that is, pronounced resonantly, almost chanted, syllable by syllable, in a tone you can feel physically in your body. This vibration usually occurs in your throat and chest. If you feel it in your face, this is singing, not vibrating. (Real experts can direct the vibration to any part of the body.) I find it easiest to vibrate in a low tone.

JHVH, when spoken, is usually vibrated as it is spelled in Hebrew: *Yod heh vav he.* There's a tendency to pronounce the *vav* as *vo,* probably because it rhymes with *Yod.* Pronounce this aloud, and you get something very similar to the traditional pagan salute, *IO EVOHE.*

Ratzkiel is the Archangel of Chokmah. The angels which carry out Ratzkiel's directions are the Auphanim, the Wheels, a name full of symbolism. The Wheel of Life. The Wheel of the Year. The invention of the wheel represents one of humankind's first uses *of* natural forces (gravity, inertia) instead of fighting against them. The Briatic Correspondence of this Sphere is "revolution," the act of revolving.

In the Old Testament, Ezekiel saw, among other things, "wheels" in a vision. Isn't it possible that what he saw was not a wheel as we know it (nor a spaceship, for that matter), but a choir of "auphanim," and that the special meaning was lost in translation? In support of this theory is the fact that Ezekiel also saw "living creatures" who bore the likenesses of an eagle, an ox, a lion and a man. Put the word "holy" in front of "living creatures" and you have the angelic army of Kether. A few lines later, Ezekiel refers to the "likeness of a throne." Thrones are the angels of Binah, the sphere which follows Chokmah.

The Spiritual Experience of this sphere is the "Vision of God Face to Face" or "Vision of the Source We Seek." This is another experience that we do not usually have while incarnate.

Chokmah represents pure force, and as such, total formlessness. If we identified completely with total formlessness, we could not remain in a form. Considering the spiritual advancement necessary to reach and identify with this sphere, it is unlikely we would be able to have this experience while in a body. Most of mankind can barely look themselves squarely in the face— much less face the Ultimate. There may be exceptions, however. Stories found in various religious myths of "ascensions" could tell of such occurrences.

The Deities found in Chokmah are of three types, each reflecting a facet of this sphere. All Great Father Gods go here: Odin, the Dagda, Olorun, Zeus/Jupiter (especially Jupiter who seems to have fathered half the population of the Mediterranean). Dius Pitar (say that ten times very quickly) belongs here, as does the father aspect of Yahveh.

The Priapic Gods are also attributed to this sephira, for Chokmah represents the absolute in the ability to fertilize— fertility in its most abstract form, far from the physical. One of the symbols for Chokmah is the penis, long venerated in ancient cultures as a symbol of the dynamic life force. This is the Great God Pan, not Pan the satyr, although this does not imply that physical sex and fertility are less holy than this spiritual fertility. We simply have not reached the realm of physical manifestation yet.

The ancient truth, "That which is above is as that which is below, but after another manner," certainly applies here. Physical fertility is a reflection, a more concrete form, of the fertility of Chokmah, just as the union of man and woman is a joining of the Lord and Lady. Neither is more holy—they are simply manifestations of the same thing on different planes.

Because Chokmah is called "Wisdom," one can attribute Pallas Athene here, as well as Isis-Urania, Vishnu, and Kwan Yin.

The Magical Image of Chokmah is a bearded male figure—The Father, Jung's Archetypal Old Man.

The Virtue is Devotion. Having seen your Source, what else could you feel, with what else be filled?

Chokmah is half of the first pair on the Tree of Life. Each pair must always be considered as two spheres together, in relation to each other. As it is impossible to understand one without the other, let us move across the Tree to Binah, the other half of the first pair.

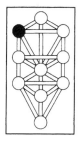

5

LISTEN TO THE
WORDS OF THE
GREAT MOTHER

Much learning does not teach understanding.
—Heraclitus[1]

MANY BOOKS OF THE Mystical Qabala say that each of the spheres emanates from the one before. Pagans may have a problem with this, because Binah is the sphere of the Goddess, and they are not going to like the implication of the Goddess emanating from the God. Other sources say that all spheres emanate from the Ain Soph at the same time; they are all one, all part of each other. Remember that even this wonderful gift to mankind, the Tree of Life, is an abstraction, man struggling to express the inexpressible, and a poor representation of what truly is, especially at this level.

Binah is the sphere whose name means "Understanding" or "Intelligence." Use your intelligence and understanding so that you won't miss the marvels of the Qabala by objecting to the way it is described.

Binah represents negativity, receptivity, passivity. It is form, force in pattern. Its color is black, a color in which all light rays are absorbed and none reflected. Without black, the absence of reflected light rays, there are no visual patterns. Without Binah, there are no forms.

---

[1] Heraclitus, *On the Universe,* fragment 16, in *Butler's Familiar Quotations* (Boston: Little Brown, 16th edition, 1992), p. 62.

The Planetary Attribution of Binah is Saturn, known as the "Restrictor." Form *is* restriction, a very necessary one. Steam with no restriction accomplishes nothing; restricted, it can power an engine. When we cast a magic circle, part of its purpose is to create a limited area in which to work, to concentrate our energies within the restriction of the circle rather than try to control the energies of the entire room.

Binah is also resistance, a springboard. If you've ever tried to push anything through water that was over your head, you'll appreciate the value of resistance. Those of you with a military bent can compare Binah to the thrust block so necessary to the workings of big cannons.

On a less impersonal level, Binah is the Goddess, the Great Mother, the Womb of Life, the Cauldron of Cerridwen. She sits at the head of the Feminine Pillar, the Pillar of Form, of Restriction.

All Great Mother Goddesses are in Binah, obviously: Isis, Danu, Demeter, Yemanja, Frigga—and goddesses which represent the feminine aspect: Sakti, Maya, Kwan Yin. Because of the Saturn aspect, Bran is placed here, although he goes equally well in other spheres.

For several reasons, I would place the god/desses of the Underworld in this sphere. The "dead" are also the unborn, and therefore the Womb of Life would be the place not only of the beginning of life, but also of its end. At the end of an incarnation, we return to Binah, divested on the way through Geburah of those things to be left behind, are broken down and, after a time, reborn. It seems only logical that the sphere of form, the first supernal inkling of form, would equate to that.

The Illusion of Binah is Death—for after Binah (working up the Tree) is Chokmah, pure force without form. Just as leaving the body is considered death, so might leaving this Idea of Form seem as death to some. But we are immortal, eternal, part of all that is. We do not die, we only change.

The Spiritual Experience of this sephira is the "Vision of Sorrow." This is the kind of sorrow most of us are not likely to experience, simply because we could not bear it. This is Isis, searching for the pieces of her mutilated husband, Mary at the foot of the Cross, Branwen betrayed and enslaved by her husband, Demeter weeping for Persephone. This vision is, perhaps, seeing through the eyes of the Goddess—seeing that through which you must struggle in order to grow. It is the pain the Lady feels when we weep.

The Lady knows, as parents do, that we must make our own mistakes in order to learn, and that mistakes often bring pain. She would spare us the pain if She could, but She can't, and so She weeps with us, sorrows with us.

Can you imagine that? Can you imagine the sorrow She carries? I'm not sure I want to try. Our own sorrows are hard enough; sharing the pain of billions upon billions is too awful to contemplate. Yet we will, one day, at some stage in our growth, know this shared sorrow. We will know, too—perhaps before then—that our own sorrow is lessened because She weeps.

I had an experience while writing this chapter that might demonstrate how potent the correspondences of the Qabala can be. "The Vision of Sorrow" brought to my mind a quote from *The Prophet:* "The deeper that sorrow carves into your being, the more joy you can contain."[2] Then I remembered a line from the television show *Kung Fu:* "I seek only to be a cup, empty of myself, filled with Oneness." Cup . . . chalice . . . cauldron . . . water . . . sea . . . the great seas of the world . . . source of life . . . womb of life . . . Binah. I looked back at my notes and saw that another name for Binah is "Marah, the Great Sea."

Binah's angels are the Aralim, the Thrones (see figure 16, page 28). One alternate title for Binah is Khorsia, the Throne. Isis (Aset in Ancient Egyptian) means "throne" and her symbol in hieroglyphs is a throne.

Although most of us will not experience the Vision of Sorrow completely in this lifetime, no life is without its sorrow, its trials. Sorrow is, unfortunately, one of the best teachers, and we learn most through our difficult times. It is said that we are never given any trial without being given strength to bear it,

[2] Kahlil Gibran, *The Prophet* (New York: Alfred A. Knopf, 1923), p. 29.

and the Aralim are the source of that strength. A throne, on the physical plane, is a large, often massive, chair—sturdy and stable. It is usually mounted on an even sturdier platform. We can imagine being curled up in a huge chair, surrounded by it, feeling its stability and strength; we are held safe, though the very world is shaken.

Over the Aralim is Tzafkiel, the Archangel of Binah. He is the Keeper of the Akashic Records, where all the days of our lives are recorded, the lessons we've learned, and those we have yet to learn. He is also the Archangel of the Archetypal Temple. I always have this vision of an open-air temple in the clouds. All the prayers and sounds of worship of all the people of all religions of all time reach this beautiful place in the form of music—each belief a different note, all blending and harmonizing into a mighty and incredibly lovely melody, ever changing and ever glorious. I can almost hear it. Listen!

Tzafkiel cares for this temple, guards it, and guides all sincere religious fellowships.

The Magical Image of Binah is a matron, a mature woman, the Goddess as Mother and/or Crone. Both are appropriate. Two of Binah's titles are "Ama," the dark, sterile mother, and "Aima," the bright fertile mother. Aima gives us birth on our descent to physical matter, incarnation. Ama receives us as we return to suffer the greater death of Self, striving ever toward oneness.

In these two names, by the way, we find an example of temura. "Ama" becomes "Aima" with the addition of the letter "yod," which is itself a symbol of fertility.

The Name of Power of Binah is *Yahveh Elohim*, usually translated as "the Lord God," which is not only inappropriate, but inaccurate. *Elohim* comes from *Eloah*, which is a feminine word, and *Him*, which is a masculine plural ending. A more accurate translation would be "the Goddess." Vibrate "Yahveh Elohim" and think "Mother." You won't be wrong. You will know what the sphere represents . . . and all will be well.

Binah's Vice is Avarice, Greed—a very negative aspect of receptivity and in-gathering, clutching all you gather to yourself.

One well-known witch, when asked the difference between meditation and prayer, answered that prayer was talking to the gods; meditation was listening to them. Binah is very much involved with meditation, for its Virtue is Silence. When you are talking, you are not listening. Silence is being receptive, allowing the inward flow to enter freely.

The following exercise is an unusual form of meditation on this Virtue. It is not easy to do, but you will find the effects very interesting.

The exercise requires the cooperation of a friend or two, and it will only work if done in the presence of others. To practice the exercise, simply do this: do not speak for at least four, and preferably six to eight, hours.

The first hour or two will be difficult. You'll be bursting with ideas, answers, comments. Be still. Eventually you'll see results. Because you are not going to make a response to what is being said, you will listen in a way you've never experienced, hear more than before, understand the value of silence. You will also find it relaxing, because you are freed from the responsibility of responding. Nothing is expected of you.

Chokmah and Binah are the states represented by the Tai Chi'n symbol, the yin and the yang. They are primal force and primal form, the ideas of force and form, masculine and feminine, active and passive, positive and negative. Between these two spheres, the Great Father and the Great Mother, is spun the web of life. They are the ebb and the flow, the coming and going, the gathering-in and the going-out. One is of no consequence without the other, for nothing can be built, or even be, without force *and* form.

The joining of the two, of God and Goddess, is that which is symbolized by the Great Rite, when in truth (actual sex) or in token, when a blade is lowered (reverently, I hope) into a chalice of wine.

This rite is often a subject of discussion among Craft people. Is one form of the ceremony more valid than another? It is my feeling that the answer is "No." Both are symbolic acts, and therefore equally valid. They are both ways of showing what happens when Chokmah and Binah interact.

There are lesbians and gays who have expressed concern about this ceremony because, they say, it represents a heterosexual act, and therefore is difficult for them to relate to. I can understand that, but please, consider this: Sex is a very good analogy for the joining of force and form, of energy and pattern, but it is *only* an analogy. Unfortunately, some people mistake the symbol for the actuality it represents. In the physical world, the bodies for new beings are created through the physical union of male and female.

The Great Rite does not symbolize human sex. It symbolizes something far greater than that. It is our way of showing that interaction between Chokmah and Binah which results in the creation of being. Disputes about who holds the cup, or whether those performing the ceremony should be fertile, or even what gender they should be reduces the rite to mere physical practice, and it loses the mighty significance it should have.

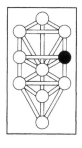

THERE SHALL YE ASSEMBLE

6

I want the seals of power and place,
The ensigns of command,
Charged by the people's unbought grace,
To rule my native land.
Nor crown, nor scepter would I ask
But from my country's will,
By day, by night, to ply the task
Her cup of bliss to fill.

—John Quincy Adams[1]

THE THREE SPHERES we have discussed so far are called The Supernal Triangle, and they represent potential. Chesed, the second sphere on the Pillar of Force, is the first sphere to represent actuality. Its name means "mercy" or "grace," and it is also known as Gedulah, or "greatness."

Here we find the benevolent ruler gods: Zeus/Jupiter, Indra, Amoun, Osiris. As you can see already, a deity can easily fit into more than one sphere. As you continue to read, you will find yourself placing others.

Chesed's Planetary Attribution is Jupiter, the Expander. In astrology, Jupiter is referred to as a benefic planet, unlike Saturn, which precedes it, and Mars, which follows it. Times are changing, but modern-day society seems to call that which is easy and peaceful "benefic" and that which is difficult and requires some effort "malefic." We pagans have learned, however,

---

[1]John Quincy Adams, "The Wants of Man," stanza 22.

that difficulties are lessons, opportunities for growth, and if they cannot honestly be greeted with cries of joy, they can at least be accepted and understood. Difficulties, however, are more appropriately discussed in the next chapter.

Chesed is a sphere that *can* provide help for those difficulties. It is called the "Hall of the Masters," the "Sphere of the Adepts." It is in Chesed, according to tradition, that those souls who have reached a certain stage in their development stop, by choice, and remain in order to be of help to those still struggling toward growth. These souls are often referred to as the Ascended Masters. In my tradition, we call them the Ancient Ones.

The Magical Image of Chesed is "A wise and kindly king upon a throne." This king is the father of his people, building industry, fostering learning, patronizing the arts. His kingdom is at peace. He is nurturing, expansion, and order. Osiris, for example, taught his people the way of agriculture, organized growing, a more stable form of life than nomadism. Chesed is the sphere of order, the first cohesion of force affected by form, on a very subtle archetypal level.

Chesed's Spiritual Experience is the "Vision of Love"; indeed, "Love" is often used as an alternate name for this sphere. The Experience can be called the "Understanding of Perfect Love." Chesed emanates from Binah, Understanding, and the two are inseparable; there cannot be love without understanding, and true understanding must bring love. This is love without judgment, without assessment, love of that which is within all creation, of that which we share, each of us, love of and from the God and Goddess. It is a total recognition of the God/dess within ourselves and others, recognition of our oneness. It is the ability to see past all the layers with which we humans cover ourselves, for Chesed is beyond human, beyond incarnation.

In certain magical lodges, the grade given to one who has reached Chesed in that long climb back up the Tree is "Adeptus Exemptus," who is exempt from the Wheel of Life, of physical incarnation. Surely one who has reached this level, one who is so close to that from which we all come is capable of a forgiveness, an understanding, that is Perfect Love.

It is highly improbable that the grade "Adeptus Exemptus" would be given to one who was still incarnate, but not impossible. However, I've met many people who "confided" to me that this was their "last life," and none of them had the qualities that one would expect in such an advanced soul.

The Virtue of this sphere is Obedience, but not the blind obedience of a slave. No proper teacher of the Western esoteric traditions would teach students to obey without question, without thought. A true teacher prepares students for independence, for the use of the mind and logical processes. Spiritual advancement is the students' own responsibility, after all, and no teacher can make that advancement for them. One large difference between Craft and Christianity is that we have no one "saving" us. All we accomplish must be through our own efforts, although we are helped from time to time, and help others when we are able. (We don't have any devil to blame our failures on, either!)

We must bring about our own advancement. Yet, as that growth occurs, students may find themselves doing exactly what the teacher wished, but because the students have decided it is the proper thing to do, not because the teacher wished it. "Obedience" at Chesed is having your own will so aligned with that of the God/dess that it is impossible for you to do other than they wish, because your wish is the same as theirs. This is not forced agreement, forced obedience. When Chesed is reached in spiritual growth, the Will *will* be that of the Lord and Lady, because it is right.

Striving for this attunement, and perhaps even believing you have achieved it to some degree, can result in the Illusion of this sphere, "self-righteousness." Sadly, many of those in less exalted states are prone to this. After all, if your will is attuned to the Gods, you must be right, right?

The Vice of Chesed is any corruption of power, or of those in power: bigotry, hypocrisy, gluttony, tyranny. Don't you think those guilty of these vices believe they are right? The bigots I've known were absolutely convinced, not only that they were right, but that God agreed with them. Tyrants believe they have a perfect right to be tyrannical.

Obviously, there is a great need for the Obligation of Chesed, Humility. For me, this is the knowledge that I am no more (and no less) than anyone else. If others are as valuable as you are, you cannot be a bigot, or a tyrant.

The Name of Power of this sphere is "El," God.

The Chasmalim, the Brilliant Ones, are Chesed's angels and they are led by Tzadkiel, Archangel of Chesed. This archangel and these angels are especially helpful to those suffering from instability of any kind: spiritual, mental or emotional.

The animal which represents Chesed is the Unicorn. Concentration on a symbol of a sphere can bring contact with that sphere, and the upsurge in the popularity of the unicorn could be an unconscious (and in many cases, conscious) invocation of the powers of Chesed. This is noteworthy in present times when world events are so definitely more indicative of Geburah, the next sphere, than they are of Chesed. Chesedic influences are usually pleasant, easy to take; Geburah is not so pleasant. Do not make the mistake of thinking this means Chesed is always "good" and Geburah is "bad." Far from it.

Exploring Geburah will help you to understand Chesed better.

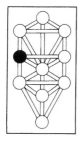

7

AND YE SHALL
BE FREE

> *Strong is the soul, and wise, and beautiful;*
> *The seeds of godlike power are in us still;*
> *Gods are we, bards, saints, heroes, if we will!*
> —Matthew Arnold[1]

THE SEPHIRA GEBURAH, "Might" (Power, Strength), is also known as Din, "Judgment," and Pachad, "Fear," all of which seem to bode ill for any dealings with this sphere. The actions of Geburah *can* be difficult, but it is not a "malefic" sphere.

Paganfolk have a better understanding of the actions of this sphere than many others in the modern world. An "easy life" with no hardships, no trials, all wishes fulfilled, and so forth, would be a sign of blessing to many. We pagans would consider it restful, but such a life seldom contributes anything to total growth. As I mentioned in the previous chapter, we might not give joyful welcome to the trials and tribulations of life, but we can accept them for the lessons they contain, the growth they make possible.

One of the things I lost (without regret) when I came to the Craft was that heart-rending cry into the darkness, "Why?" There was usually no answer, not even an echo. I might not receive an answer even now, but I no longer cry into the darkness. I *know* there is a reason, and that I will eventually understand.

---

[1] Matthew Arnold, written in a copy of *Emerson's Essays* (London: *The Oxford Dictionary of Quotations*, 1923), p. 15.

I am not afraid of the influences of Geburah. They are an integral part of the workings of the Goddess, and as necessary to all existence as is Chesed.

The "fear" reflected in the title "Pachad" is better translated as "awe," especially awe of natural forces. It is the feeling you get watching films of Mt. St. Helens as it erupts, or when you see "before and after" pictures of some cataclysmic event. It is also the wonderful feeling depicted in the lovely scene from Kenneth Grahame's *Wind in the Willows*, when Rat and Mole find themselves in the presence of Pan:

> All this he saw, for one moment breathless and intense, vivid on the morning sky; and still, as he looked, he lived; and still as he lived, he wondered. "Rat!" he found breath to whisper, shaking "Are you afraid?"
>
> "Afraid?" murmured the Rat, his eyes shining with unutterable love. "Afraid of *Him?* O, never, never! And yet—and yet—O, Mole, I am afraid!"[2]

The term "God-fearing" should mean this, not abject terror of a power that will strike you with a lightning bolt at the slightest transgression.

The Magical Image of this sphere is a "Mighty warrior in his chariot," or her chariot if you prefer; a warrior queen is an acceptable and possibly more ancient image. While the benevolent king in Chesed rules and nurtures, the warrior king of Geburah defends and punishes. Many ancient kings were in front of their soldiers as they charged into battle. Statues of Egyptian Pharaohs held a crook and flail; the crook to guide their people and the flail to punish transgressors. These statues reflect an understanding of the need for balance between Chesed and Geburah in the rhythm of life.

Geburah's Planetary Attribution is, of course, Mars; and Geburah, like Mars is so easily misunderstood. It represents de-

---

[2] Kenneth Grahame, *The Wind in the Willows* (New York: Tor Books, 1989), p. 138.

struction, the breaking down of form. White blood cells perform Geburic function in your body, your inner kingdom. The surgeon who removes a cancer or lances an abscess does the same.

Consider the Grand Canyon, result of millions of years of wearing down, or destruction of form, and tell me that such a glorious thing is the result of something malefic. Another, less obvious but equally valid, example is the London Fire. The destruction of life and property is awful to contemplate, but remember, the fire occurred at the height of the plague. Rats bearing the disease-carrying fleas were abundant in the slums, most of which were destroyed by the fire, thus wiping out the source of the plague. Without this destruction, the whole of Europe might have been devastated, not to mention what could have happened to the population of England.

Consider, in more recent times, another piece of physical breaking-down — the destruction of the Berlin Wall! And what about the break-up of the U.S.S.R? Oh, yes, there are myriad difficulties as the various countries struggle with their newly regained independence, but surely the good aspects of this can be seen.

The rhythm on which the Craft places so much emphasis is an integral part of the workings of the Qabala, as seen by a strong emphasis on the ebb and flow of energies between the three pairs of spheres. It is foolish to ignore Geburah's place in the scheme of things, because we live with it every day. We are dealing with Geburah every time we eat. Our food is broken down, releasing energy for our bodies. The form of the food is sacrificed to release the life force you must have to live. Yes, *sacrificed*, for sacrifice is nothing more than the destruction of form to release force.

We do this every time we burn a candle, start a car, turn up a heater. In ancient times of blood sacrifice, the body was destroyed to release the life force within. We no longer make blood sacrifices (except at the Blood Bank), but we are still involved with the forces of Geburah every moment we live, and thereafter.

At this point in our discussion of the Universal Tree, let us consider the earthly tree. It grows in its proper season, and in the Autumn the leaves change color and die, falling to the ground. There, in the natural course of events, they break down, become part of the earth, and nourish the very tree that produced them. This is Nature's way. The tree becomes larger and stronger in its Chesed cycle *because* of its Geburah cycle.

Unless, of course, some fool carts the leaves away and burns them, thereby not only depriving the tree of its rightful nourishment, but polluting the air as well. This idiot pays for this stupidity by ending up with a starving tree, or spending a fortune on chemical fertilizers to replace that which Mother Nature would have provided herself, if left alone. If a garden *must* be neat, the gathered leaves should be placed in a compost heap which not only allows, but encourages, the Geburah of Nature to work. Organic gardeners understand Geburah.

Why is the rest of the world so afraid of Geburah that they even deny its existence? Our bodily secretions and excretions rid our bodies of things which are useless and/or dangerous. The ancient Romans, knowing as they did that this function is as holy as any other, even had a goddess who ruled over the natural excretions of the body.

Today, our very laws reflect this fear. All during our lives, we eat food which has drawn its nourishment directly or indirectly from the Earth. When we die, do we put our bodies into the ground so that the Geburic cycle can take place? Nope. We embalm them, saving them for I don't know what, and depriving the Earth of the minerals which are rightly hers to claim.

All the energies represented by the Tree will function as they must. If blocked, they will try to burst through the blockage. With the energies of Geburah, this could result in a war, or some natural disaster . . . or several! Noticed a plethora of natural disasters lately, hmmmm?

While the war gods, such as Mars and Ares, are obvious attributions to Geburah, so also are Minerva/Athena, who became a warrior in defense of those who had been wronged, and Bran, who avenged the wrong done his sister. Kali also represents the destructive force.

I place the "smith" gods here—Brigid, Tubal Cain, Vulcan/Hephaestus—to reflect another aspect of Geburah. This sphere is called the "Hall of Karma," the "Hall of Judgment." As the smith pounds a creation into shape, plunging it again and again into the fire, bending and shaping and purifying it until it becomes a strong, perfect weapon or tool, so does the process of Karma perfect our spirits with the energies of Geburah. It never destroys that which is eternal, never the essence, but only that which is unnecessary and temporary. When we rid ourselves of unnecessary weight, we've lost nothing necessary to us, no part of our true selves. We've been freed from a burden we were carrying around unnecessarily. Breaking any bad habit frees us from its control.

I would also place the god Set here in his role as Desert Storm God. Wind-blown sand blasts things clean. Set, in this function, removes only the temporal, never the eternal.

Geburah's Virtues are Energy and Courage, both fairly obvious in view of the meaning of the sphere. Its Obligation is also Courage. The Vices are Cruelty and *Wanton* Destruction.

Imagine that you stand before a giant glacier. With a snap of your fingers, you can cause that glacier to crumble into billions of ice cubes.

Imagine that you stand on the world's highest mountain. With a whisper, you can create a hundred-mile-per-hour wind that has the power to sweep all the way around the world.

Imagine that you can, with the blink of an eyelash, destroy this planet. Imagine, if you can, controlling this kind of power. Take a few minutes.

Can you get a glimpse of that power? This is the merest hint of one aspect of the Spiritual Experience of Geburah, the "Vision of Power."

The Illusion of Geburah is Invincibility, and it is certainly understandable that undergoing the Spiritual Experience associated with Geburah could make you feel invincible.

However, when that glacier crumbles, it is going to fill that lake in front of it and send a giant wave right over the place where you are standing.

That hundred-mile-per-hour wind is going to circle the globe, destroying everything in its path, carry with it a good deal of debris (trees, people, cars, buildings), come up behind you, and remove you from that mountain with considerable force.

If you destroy the planet you are standing on . . . what goes around comes around. Karma.

The Vision of Power is a realization of the power which you can control *and* a realization of the results of and responsibility for the use of that power. This is the Hall of Karma, and never is the understanding of cause and effect so great as in this experience.

Geburah's Name of Power is Elohim Gibor, "Almighty Gods and Goddesses," or "Almighty Ones."

Several weapons and objects are symbols of Geburah. It is really interesting to note that all five-sided figures are symbolic of this sphere—including the pentagon. Is it coincidence, I wonder, that our national armed forces have their headquarters in a five-sided building called the "Pentagon"?

Geburah's Archangel is the mighty Khamael, protector of the weak, avenger of the wronged. He leads the Seraphim, the Fiery Serpents (much like the Greek Furies), in the performance of their duties—the slaying of dragons, defense of the inner country, King Arthur's "might for right".

The Golden Dawn ritual for the initiation of the Neophyte says that "Unbalanced mercy is weakness and the fading away of the will. Unbalanced Severity is cruelty and barrenness of mind."[3] Again, consider two opposites on the tree, this time Geburah and Chesed. If it seems to you that these sephiroth are on the wrong pillars, consider this: Chesed expands, Geburah restricts. Let there be power and compassion.

My husband and I are involved in an activity indicative of the balancing of Geburic and Chesedic energies: an exercise program. We are using exercises to burn off calories and free our-

---

[3] Israel Regardie, *The Complete Golden Dawn System of Magic*, Vol. 6 (Phoenix, New Falcon, 1984), p. 14.

selves from excess pounds put there by a little Chesedic gluttony, using energy to make ourselves healthy and therefore creating more energy. It takes courage to tell those aching muscles to move and will power to get in there and do it. We are breaking down form (fat) to release force (body heat and energy).

There will be a further balance eventually; this activity is not entirely Geburic and shouldn't be. Those muscles, screaming right now, will be built into strong healthy muscles. Some of that flab will be replaced by firm flesh. Geburah and Chesed will work together, balanced, as they should be.

Chesed's idealism is balanced by the realism of Geburah. They are the latent and kinetic energies of the Universe, the building up and the ebbing away of power, anabolism and catabolism, the waxing and waning Moon.

Always consider one with the other, and you will understand both much better.

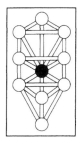

8

LET THERE
BE BEAUTY

Beauty is a pledge of the possible conformity between the soul and nature, and consequently a ground of faith in the supremacy of the good.

—George Santayana[1]

WE HAVE REACHED the center of the Tree, its heart, its pivot point, the sphere whose name means Beauty or Harmony, Tifareth. This sphere is equilibrium, the epitome of balance. Tifareth is the balance between Mercy and Severity, between active and passive, between force and form. It is the child of the God and Goddess.

Tifareth's Planetary Attribution is the Sun, center of our solar system. All planets move around the Sun in their various orbits, as the spheres are placed around Tifareth. Interesting, is it not, that the sphere which, as you will see, would be suitable for no other celestial attribution *but* the Sun, should be placed in the center of the Tree at a time when the Sun was not considered to be the center of the Universe?

Esoteric tradition holds that the power of our Sun comes from another sun. So does the power of Tifareth, called the "Lesser Countenance," reflect the power of the "Greater Countenance," Kether.

---

[1] George Santayana, *The Sense of Beauty*, Part IV, Expression (New York: Dover, 1896).

Tifareth's Pagan Mythology is multitudinous, because Tifareth has two aspects, death and rebirth. In this sphere are placed the sacrificed kings: Osiris, Llew, Dionysus, Adonis, Balder. Also placed here are the sacred children: Horus, Jesus, Gwern, Lugh, and others. Because of the solar attribution of Tifareth, the Sun being symbolic of life, light, healing, and illumination, you find healing gods, Sun deities (Ra, Apollo, Rama, Amaterasu) and the givers of illumination (Krishna, Buddha, Mithra, and others) here also.

Another Tifareth figure from mythology, although not a deity, is King Arthur. According to legend, Arthur advocated the use of force for protection of those who needed it—might *for* right—instead of might *is* right. That *idea* is Geburic, but the advancement in ideas, the illumination, is an aspect of Tifareth. The bringers of illumination are not necessarily religious figures. They are those who attempt to teach better ways to do things and try to help humanity better its lot. Osiris is revered not only as a God, but as a man who taught his people agriculture. Gandhi was a man, not a god, but he very definitely offered a new way of thinking, and Dr. Martin Luther King carried on his tradition. Each of us will have others in mind who have Tifareth qualities. The ones I've mentioned have one other thing in common. They were murdered. They often are.

There are two Spiritual Experiences of Tifareth, just as there are two aspects. The first is "The Vision of the Harmony of Things," the knowledge that the Universe is unfolding as it should. It is the Tao. Those who have truly experienced this are often removed from ordinary irritations and worries, because they have seen the harmony, the big picture, and they understand there is reason for all.

Now, this does *not* mean that they understand that everything that happens day to day is the result of something in a former life. "Whoa!" someone will say when your wallet is stolen, "you must have stolen from him in another life. Bad Karma, man!"

Horsefeathers. *Karma* means "evolution," not retribution. Karmic lessons are spiritual ones. What spiritual lesson is learned by having your wallet stolen? There are people still messing up things in this life. Having your wallet stolen means that the thief has lessons to learn, not you. Those who self-righteously spout the "bad karma" nonsense do so because they want to believe it. After all, if it is your fault, it can't happen to them.

The understanding gained through Tifareth is much greater than that, and deals with much larger issues. When you begin to look at things from a Qabalistic point of view, you'll ponder the advancement of people, wonder which experiences they've had, where they would be on the Tree. In modern history, I believe that Gandhi had seen the Vision of the Harmony of Things, or come close. His priorities seem to reflect that. He believed that how a person worshipped was not important; self-respect was, and understanding was, but status was not. Gandhi-ji was not a saint—I'm told he was a rotten father—but he taught another way of thinking, a more mature way, and one that exhibited a rare kind of courage.

Jesus of Nazareth is probably the most modern of the sacrificed kings. The Adeptus Minor Ritual, the Tifareth initiation in magical lodges, was a ritual death and burial (simulated of course). We are all familiar with Jesus' death . . . an Adeptus Minor ritual that was not a simulation. For those of us who have become Craft after being raised Christian, Jesus remains a great teacher who taught many things with which we can easily agree.

Gandhi may also have had the second Spiritual Experience of Tifareth, and certainly Jesus did. I express this experience as "Understanding the Mysteries of Sacrifice." It is usually called "Understanding of the Mysteries of the Crucifixion," but crucifixion is only one form of sacrifice, and contemplation on any of the sacrificed kings, whatever their manner of death, should bring results.

Pagans of all traditions are accused of barbaric blood sacrifices, and the accusations were true at one time. True, not only of nature religions, but of Judaism and Christianity. What people today do not understand is the attitude of the Sacred King, the meaning of his sacrifice. Believing, as they did, that the present life was only one of many, these kings did not fear the death of the body. They offered that body, the life force it contained, and the personality they possessed at that time, as gifts to the gods and to their people, believing that this sacrifice advanced them spiritually. Their next life would be better, and the present life of the people they represented would be better. This presents a far different picture from that of unwilling sacrifice, screaming, and cursing. In unwilling sacrifice, energy is released, it is true, but not the kind of energy that is beneficial.

We have learned, I think, other ways to give to the gods, ways that do not involve the release of life force, ways I believe are better.

Imagine, if you will, that you are the God or the Goddess. Here comes someone lugging the body of one of your children slung over his shoulder. He throws it at your feet, and proudly announces he's brought you a gift. How would you feel about that?

There are other ways to give to Them, and some of these are much more difficult. The greatest gift you can give Them is yourself, and that is the only life sacrifice you have the right to give.

No, I do not mean that you should commit suicide in Their Honor. Don't be ridiculous. What would that accomplish, other than to show an extreme disrespect for the life you've been given?

In Sothistar's Second Degree, we give our lives to the Gods to do with as they will. From that point on, our lives are dedicated to Their service. Does this mean we don't have everyday lives? No. It simply means that the Gods come first. Unless we really fight against it, we'll be led in the ways They want us to go. They lead me to teach and write. They will lead others in different ways.

Willing sacrifice means that we are aware that everything we do must be done with Them in mind. We should try to conduct ourselves in ways that make Them proud, that do Them honor. The word *sacrifice* means "to make holy." Consider that; meditate on it, and all that it can mean.

There are three Magical Images for Tifareth: A king, a child, and a sacrificed god. The one you choose depends on the aspect of Tifareth you wish to contact.

In my tradition, as in others, both second and third degree initiations relate to Tifareth. The second degree represents ritual death; the initiate dies to an old life and is reborn to a life of service to the Goddess and her Lord. Then comes a time of spiritual testing. When this period is over, the Third Degree is invoked, to celebrate the rebirth of the High Priest or High Priestess.

Authorities will give one or two archangels for Tifareth — Michael or Raphael. Raphael is appropriate because he is the Archangel of Air, and Tifareth is on the Middle Pillar, the Air Pillar. He is also the Healing Archangel, and Tifareth is the sphere of healing. But Tifareth is also the sphere of the Sun, and Michael is the Archangel of Fire, having some healing aspects as well.

Once again, our filing cabinet analogy comes to our rescue. The archangel you work with should be the one most applicable to the work you are doing. There is ample room in your drawer for more than one archangel file folder.

Yahveh Eloah Va Daath, "God/dess made manifest in the sphere of the mind is the Name of Power for Tifareth. Its Virtue is "Devotion to the Great Work," dedication to the deliberate evolution of your soul. Its Vice is Pride. Do not confuse pride with self-respect in this instance. Tifareth's Vice might be better expressed as "false pride," or "lack of humility".

We are all part of the Lord and Lady; they are within us. To consider ourselves unworthy of respect would be to dishonor Them within us. However, they are within *all* of us, and having worked to achieve Tifareth consciousness does not make you a better person than anyone else. Humility can be expressed thus: "I am no more and no less than you." To have humility does not mean to be a doormat; it means recognition of the equality of the God and Goddess within, and within others. Those who have not reached Tifareth are not inferior, any more than are children who are chronologically younger.

The Illusion of Tifareth fits rather neatly with its Vice. Tifareth's Illusion is Identification—identifying yourself by what you do, not who you are.

Who are you? What are the first three things that come to mind? The first answer is probably your name, but what about the other two? Did they include your job? Your religion? Your political affiliation? Your status in your coven?

That's a problem—identifying yourself with what you do, with a group, or with a set of beliefs.

What if your political party or job or coven went away?

Some people believe in "world changes"—disasters so great that little civilization is left on Earth. What if this happened? Where's your fancy job? Your money? Your status? Your political party? Your clothes? Your fancy ritual equipment? Those who believe in world changes also say this: Only those whose sense of self-worth is not connected to their job or mundane status survive the aftermath of such a change.

It does not take a world change, however, for one's world to shake. I am aware of a lady who had followed one of the major traditions for decades. Many years ago, however, she became disillusioned with others of her tradition, and withdrew from that community. She continued to practice and teach her tradition, following it faithfully.

Recently, however, through the Internet, she found that others who bore the name of her tradition were following a path quite different from hers. When she found that her practices were unlike any others of that tradition, she finally sought out her High Priestess, and demanded the truth.

The truth truly shook her world. The truth was that *years* before the lady I speak of joined the coven, her teacher, in disapproval of that tradition's practices, had left its path and its teachings. This in itself is not a bad thing. It's been done before and since, and will be done again. The problem is that the teacher didn't tell her students that she no longer followed or taught the tradition in question. She still doesn't tell them. She lets them think they are following this tradition.

Can you imagine what my friend felt? The majority of her life had been based on a lie. The tradition she had followed for many years did not have the name she thought it had. If her sense of self-worth had been based on her pride in that name, she might well have crumbled. I believe that, for a while, she thought she would.

She didn't. She realized that it was not the name of the tradition that made her who she was. It was not the practice of that tradition. Her life was rooted in the gods and her relationship with them. Her roots were fine, only the trappings, the name, had been stripped away, and so was found to be really unimportant.

My friend already possessed the quality necessary to overcome false pride, the Vice of Tifareth. That quality, the Obligation of Tifareth, is Integrity.

In addition to its definition of honesty, integrity also means completeness. It is my feeling that this is not so much a matter of becoming complete, as it is a matter of recognizing exactly what you require to be complete. And even more important, of realizing what is *not* necessary to your completeness. It is here, working in Tifareth, that I believe you become aware of what is truly the essence of yourself.

One animal attributed to Tifareth—the Phoenix—expresses much of what the sphere represents. The Phoenix dies in flame and is reborn from its own ashes, again and again. Another animal attributed to Tifareth is the pelican. The pelican is depicted in heraldry as taking flesh from her breast to feed her young—surely an excellent symbol of sacrifice. Together, these two represent both spiritual experiences of Tifareth.

The Briatic Correspondence of Tifareth is Wholeness or Centrality. This is most suitable for a sphere which is at the very center of the Tree, and is the most balanced sphere on the Tree.

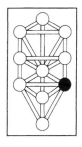

9

FOR BEHOLD, ALL ACTS OF LOVE AND PLEASURE ARE MY RITUALS

The growth of the mind is the widening of the range of consciousness, and . . . each step forward has been a most painful and laborious achievement.

—C. G. Jung[1]

THE NEXT SPHERE, Netzach, lies on the Pillar of Force and represents "Victory"—victory in the sense of achievement. In my coven, which uses the Tree of Life as a framework for development, it is after work with Netzach that a student reaches First Degree. This requires so much work and time that it truly does represent quite an achievement.

Netzach is emotion, love in all forms. Its Pagan Mythology includes Venus, Aphrodite, Hathor, and Rhiannon. Its Planetary Attribution is, naturally, Venus. This makes Netzach seemingly easy to understand, but this is not necessarily so.

The Archangel of this sphere is Haniel, who is a patron of the arts. His angels are the Elohim. As you've learned, this word can be translated as "goddesses/gods." How can gods and goddesses be angels? They are not, of course. What is represented here is the energy of the image we have given each deity in our mind. It is in Netzach that the pure deity energy is actually broken into the various aspects of the Lord and Lady with which you are familiar—the *energy*, that is, not the forms; they come later. Netzach is like a prism which divides light into rainbow colors.

---

[1] C. G. Jung, *Contributions to Analytical Psychology* (1928), ¶340.

Perhaps I should explain here my own view of the Universe. Some see Wicca as a duotheistic religion, this is, a religion which teaches there is one God and one Goddess of whom all others are aspects.

Others see each of the deities as separate individuals— Hecate is not the Morrigan, is not Kali.

I don't fit in either category. I believe there is a Oneness, and that it includes *everything*—gods, goddesses, planets, trees, birds, worms—everything, including humankind. The gods and goddesses are a part of that Oneness, and they are as individual as we are.

I heard another way of expressing this on the television show *Babylon 5*. One of the alien characters, a Minbari, was explaining their spiritual philosophy. Briefly, it was this: The Universe is alive, and souls are a part of that life, sent out in order to learn. We are the Universe trying to learn about itself.

We came down the Tree (or up it, if you prefer) to learn, and are working our way home, back to the Source, learning and growing and taking that with us.

It is my feeling, therefore, that the different colors revealed by the prism of Netzach are not only the gods, but everything else, as well.

Netzach's Spiritual Experience is the "Vision of Beauty Triumphant." All of us have touched this experience when, in a moment of great, almost unbearable beauty, we have glimpsed infinity. Having known such a moment, this experience is a knowledge that the harmony, the beauty of Tifareth will triumph. If you have touched such a moment, briefly, imagine the glory of a complete Spiritual Experience in this sphere.

Netzach's Name of Power is "Yahveh Tzabaoth." Never mind how it translates. What it means is the opposite of "E Pluribus Unum," "out of the many, one." It means "out of the one, many," all the facets of the God and Goddess as seen in all their glorious ways.

Netzach lies at the base of the Masculine Pillar, and is chock full of goddesses. How so? This is one of the reasons I prefer to call this pillar the Pillar of Force. Netzach is energy, creative energy, the energy you put into rituals to make them effective. The form of the rituals themselves comes under Hod, the next sphere.

This sphere is the spark of genius that touches us when we are being creative. It is the energy you feel when you are writing a ritual; the energy that turns it into a "given" ritual instead of a written one.

In *The White Goddess*, Robert Graves spends 500 pages discussing the fact that no poet deserves the name unless his poetry is directed to and inspired by the Goddess.[2] (Imagine, 500 pages about Netzach!) Graves says that the "muse" that real poets and artists credit with inspiration of their work is none other than the Triple Goddess. (We hear of nine muses now, but Mr. Graves says there is only one, "divided" by some patriarchal chauvinist in a "divide and conquer" move.) Netzach represents the spark which makes the difference between a craftsman and an artist, between a rhyme and a poem.

Oddly enough, the very presence of this creative spark can bring about the Illusion of this sphere, Projection. Artists and poets often paint or write something that expresses feelings others have. Realizing this, the creative ones come to believe that others share *all* their feelings. A little thought can reveal the kind of problems this particular illusion can cause.

Another aspect of projection is projecting your negative feelings onto others. *You* don't feel those things, *they* do. You are full of love, and peace. *They* are the ones with anger, fear, greed, etc. This means, of course, that any problems are not your fault, not your responsibility. Yeah, right.

That's a lie, and you know it, or you should know it. (I'll come back to this in a moment.)

The Virtue of Netzach is Unselfishness. Naturally, love, true love, would be unselfish. Netzach's Vice is Unchastity. This is not an attempt to impose upon you the ethics of another religion. Unchastity, or impurity do not necessarily relate to your sex life. Motives can be impure, as well.

---

[2] Robert Graves, *The White Goddess* (Winchester, MA: Faber & Faber, 1947).

In order to overcome the Vice of Unchastity, you must first learn about yourself. In our tradition, you would have worked up to Netzach through the spheres between it and Malkuth, and learned a great deal about yourself in the process. This isn't always easy. One of the things you must learn is self-responsibility. We are responsible for everything we do, say, think, or feel. *We* are, not the devil, not the other guy. You.

For example, no one "makes" you mad. You allow someone to irritate you. Don't try to blame someone else. Don't try to deny you have those feelings, either. You have them. You get angry, you get hurt. You're human. There are times when you have every right to feel the way you do, but even when your feelings are unreasonable, don't deny you have them. Don't lie to yourself; that is the worst kind of lie.

Lying, especially to yourself, makes your mind, your being, impure, in my opinion. Blaming others for what you feel is also an impurity. You must take responsibility for all you are, all you do, all you think, and feel. If you don't like what you are, change it! The Obligation of this sphere, responsibility, will help you overcome the Vice of Unchastity *and* the Illusion of Projection.

A psychologist of my acquaintance deals (unbeknownst to her) almost entirely with Netzach energy with her patients. Although the majority of her clients are artists and writers, those who are not benefit from art therapy as well.

My psychologist friend has learned the value of positive Netzach energies—not the aspect of emotion, which, when untempered by the logic and reason of the next sphere, Hod, can result in a person totally ruled by emotion, but the *creative* energy of Netzach. In her therapy, she encourages her patients to create, especially in the visual arts (painting, sculpture, etc.). The quality of the artwork is unimportant to the therapy; the importance lies in the act of creation.

We have much better contact with Netzach when we are children, because we are freely creative. We paint, write stories and poems, and model clay solely for the joy of creating. There comes a time, however, when we become concerned with the quality of our creativity, rather than the fun of creation. We worry about whether our paintings or poems are "good" or not. If they are not, by whatever standards we choose to accept, we stop creating them, and cut ourselves off from the Netzach energy.

If you would develop Netzach contacts, get out your paints and paint a picture just for the fun of it. It doesn't matter a jot whether it is "good." Throw it away if you like. Write horrible poems, or the world's worst short story. While you are being creative, you are touching and being touched by Netzach energies and that is infinitely more important than the results that appear on paper.

These energies are a part of you and not using them is like not using one of your feet. Using them will touch every part of your life, in ways you can't imagine. I know this to be true. For various reasons, there was a long period when I didn't write. I kept busy, but had no real writing projects. Now that I'm involved in revising this book, I find things changing in other aspects of my life, changing for the better.

Don't ignore the Netzach energies in you; bring them into your life, and see the changes they bring.

We will learn more about Netzach if we study Hod.

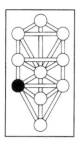

10

TO THESE SHALL I
TEACH THAT WHICH
IS AS YET UNKNOWN

If the radiance of a thousand suns were to burst forth at once in the sky, it would be like the splendor of the Mighty One.

—Bhagavad Gita[1]

ACROSS THE 27TH PATH from Netzach is Hod. Hod's name means "glory," or "splendor" and it is the sphere of the intellect. Hod represents science and teaching, and all teaching gods and messengers are attributed to this sphere. All intellectual activities of the mind are here: books, communications, esoteric teachings, the text of rituals, puns, puzzles and cryptograms.

Hod's Planetary Attribution is Mercury, the planet which receives the most light from the Sun.

The Vice of Hod is Falsehood, Dishonesty. This may or may not be deliberate falsehood; it may be dishonesty with self. When the energy of Hod begins to have an effect, you develop a tremendous talent for rationalization. Your logic, if it is not based on truth, will not be truth, but it will be wonderfully logical. Work with and in Hod can stimulate the intellect and its processes, and unfortunately, these can be used to rationalize decisions with great wit and cunning, whether or not these ideas are based on truth and right.

---

[1] *Bhagavad Gita As It Is*, 11:2, published by the Bhaktivedanta Book Trust, New York.

I have seen this self-deception manifest in very interesting and very "Hodic" ways. The student might believe that form is all—that if they do a rite in the right way at the right time and with the precise words, exact pronunciation, they don't have to worry about handling energies, developing will. There is no need to use self-discipline or take care of their minds. The edict against the use of "recreational" drugs is ridiculous. (This edict exists in my group.) Students can also get very hung up on books, etc. Only that which is printed is valid. Even typed words do not get the respect printed words do, and verbal teachings are totally discounted.

At this point, the students have not learned (or have forgotten) that wisdom and intelligence are not the same thing. The truth, they feel, is that which is worded the most eloquently (and is, of course, most correct grammatically).

This self-deception connects to the Illusion of Hod, "order." The Universe in Hod appears to have perfect order—the secret is in learning what that order is. The order will seem manifest in Hod. It's comforting to think that if you do *this*, *that* will happen. In some cases, it may be true, but not always. The Universe does indeed have perfect order, but because the Universe is much more vast and complex than we can imagine, that order is not always clear to us, or as simple as it might seem.

If we continue to learn, however, we will soon come to understand, not how the Universe works, but that it is more complicated than we thought. You'll also come to understand how little we do understand, and how much more there is to learn. If we are lucky, we will be inspired to learn even more, for "to learn" is the Obligation of Hod.

The Virtue of Hod is Truthfulness. Oh, what a difficult virtue it can be to achieve, and what a painful one! It involves not only truth with others, but must include truthfulness with self, that most difficult, most agonizing truth to bear.

The onset of this Virtue can be as disconcerting as any Vice. Some interpret "being totally honest" as "letting it all hang out," and "saying what I really feel, man." For some reason, what they "really feel" is all negative. It takes some time to realize that this truthfulness should include the positive things that are felt, and that truthfulness need not be tactless and inconsiderate.

There are two archangels attributed to Hod: Raphael and Michael. Hod is situated directly below Geburah, home of Khamael, defender of the wronged and protector of the weak. Michael is also a defender, especially on psychic planes. Raphael, however, is the healer of psychic wounds, and of Air which represents the intellect. He, therefore, has a rightful place in this sphere.

The striving for knowledge can place us in danger, psychically, and it is good at these times to have mighty Michael on your side. Should these explorations result in psychic hurts, however, it is good to have Raphael. The archangel you invoke depends, again, on the work you are doing.

The angels of Hod are the "Beni Elohim," literally "Sons of the God/dess," but better translated as "Children of God/dess." These are the forms for the energies represented by the Elohim, the angels of Netzach.

These forms are not the transient, often illusory, thought forms of Yesod, but are "telesmic images," something very different. A telesmic image is a form that has been imbued by hundreds of years of use with special qualities and a kind of permanence. Every god image can be used as a telesmic image. You visualize the form strongly, establishing it firmly on the astral plane by concentration and giving of energy. When it is established and has become a worthy vessel for that deity (or other figure) you wish to invoke, that particular energy will enter your image and it will become the God or Goddess.

Hod's Spiritual Experience is the "Vision of Splendor." Splendor in a great building, a pyramid, a vast desert, an affair of state, can bring awe, can be most impressive, even if it is not beautiful. It need not touch the heart. It does touch the mind. The Vision of Splendor reaches the mind in the same way that the Vision of Beauty Triumphant touches the heart.

The power of Shakespeare's plays, their words, their emotions, is beautiful; it touches the heart. The fact that they still do so after 400 years, the fact that a human, mortal mind was able to put words together in such a way that they are still moving today, is splendid. Yet the experience is as important and moving as the Vision of Beauty Triumphant.

The Magical Image of Hod is the Hermaphrodite. Hod and Netzach are the pair of spheres closest to physical manifestation, and at the bases of the Masculine and Feminine Pillars. We are as close to the division of the sexes as we can be without actually manifesting as such. The Hermaphrodite, being of both sexes, symbolizes that, as well as symbolizing the sphere of male deities on the Feminine Pillar.

It is said that as man can fertilize woman on the physical plane, so does woman fertilize man on the spiritual plane. Therefore, the gods are not ill-placed in this sphere. In contrast to Binah and Chokmah, with the energy of the male sphere fertilizing the female sphere, and the female sphere providing form, restriction, and organization for the male energy, Hod is fertilized by Netzach, the female energizing the male, and the male "Mind" providing form for the female "Soul."

Does the representation of Mind as male and Soul as female offend you? Why? Is one more important than the other? Does Soul advance and grow without the thoughts, ideas, the logic of Mind? Does the Mind grow and advance without the spark, the emotion, the wonder of Soul?

The art therapy I spoke of in the previous chapter, although in appearance dealing totally with Netzach, still contains a balance between Netzach and Hod. The creative energy is invoked and used to provide the impetus and inspiration for the artwork, but it is put into a form, a pattern, which is a function of Hod.

More than any other pair, Hod and Netzach are best understood by comparing them. For instance, occult books, grimoires, and studies, come under the jurisdiction of Hod, while Netzach is associated with natural magic, instinctive magic. Hod is the text of a ritual, the form, while Netzach is the performance of the ritual and the energy given to it. Hod is the drawn pentagram; Netzach, the flame when it is charged. Netzach is sound; Hod is words, sound in pattern. (Mantras especially come under the jurisdiction of Hod.) Netzach is concerned with Nature contact and elemental contacts, Hod with ritual magic and knowledge for the sake of knowledge. Hod is the printed circuit; Netzach the current that activates it. Hod is the Lord of Books; Netzach the Lady of Nature. Hod is instinct; Netzach, emotion. Hod is ceremonial magic; Netzach the traditional Craft.

Between Hod and Netzach is also the Great Rite.

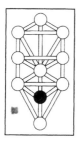

11

AND THE WHITE
MOON AMONG
THE STARS

Stepping on the moon, I begin
the gay pilgrimage to new
Jerusalems
in foreign galaxies.
—Stanley Kunitz[1]

THE SPHERE WHICH just precedes physical being is Yesod, the "Foundation." Yesod is the sphere most easily reached from physical manifestation, just as its Planetary Attribution, the Moon, is the heavenly body most easily reached from Earth.

In a sense, we live in Yesod as constantly as we live in Malkuth, for Malkuth (the next sphere) is physical matter, but Yesod provides the life in that matter.

The attribution of the Moon to Yesod means that all Moon deities belong in this sphere: Luna, Hecate, Diana, Hathor, Ganesha. The phases of the Moon reflect the faces of the Triple Goddess: Waxing, Full, Waning; Maiden, Mother, Crone. The Moon in waxing and waning phases does not truly grow or shrink. Moonrise after moonrise during the waxing moon, more of Her is revealed to us, parts of the Moon that were always there, but not illuminated. During the waning moon, more becomes hidden, moonrise after moonrise, until the Moon itself cannot be seen. Yet the physical Moon does not change during

---

[1] Stanley Kunitz, "The Flight of Apollo" in *The Poems of Stanley Kunitz 1928–1978* (Boston: Little, Brown, 1979), p. 48.

these phases. It presents, at all times, the same side, the same face. The phases are illusion, and Yesod is the Sphere of Illusion.

Yesod is the Akasha, the Astral, the Etheric Planes. It is in Yesod that we build our thoughtforms, or rather their images. We build these forms in Yesod and those images, if imbued with enough of our own energy, pull the energy into them from other spheres. Never forget, however, that the images in Yesod are just that—images. All our thoughtforms are just images until energy enters them. The Mirror and the Moon are connected with Yesod for good reason; both reflect light and images. One of Yesod's titles is "The Treasurehouse of Images." These supposed forms can be very misleading, and the uninformed are often led astray by accepting them as the real thing.

For this, among many reasons, the use of a symbolic system such as the Qabala is not only useful, but necessary. First, training the deeper levels of the mind to use the same symbols as the conscious mind can prevent a lot of misinterpretation. Secondly, the knowledge of the spheres beyond Yesod teaches us that the "images" we see are only symbols of that which is greater, that there is more to the "beyond" than the Astral Plane.

The Name of Power of Yesod is "Shaddai El Chai," usually translated "Almighty Living God." I prefer "Almighty Living One." It is an interesting name. *El* does mean "God" and *Chai* is "Life," but *Shaddai* means "breasts." I'm tempted to do a paragraph or two pondering on this name, but I think I'll leave that to you. It would make a very good meditation.

Yesod is the sexual plane and the fertility plane. It is in Yesod that souls enter the bodies created for them. This falls under the jurisdiction of the angels of this sphere, the Aishim, "Souls of Fire."

Only one other author attributes these angels to Yesod: W. G. Gray. The rest attribute the Kerubim to this sphere, and the Aishim to the next sphere, Malkuth. I have reasons for attributing the Kerubim to Malkuth, which I will explain in greater detail in the next chapter.

Just as different traditions of the Craft, and other similar beliefs, have their own attributions of the elements, their own view of the Lord and Lady, so do Qabalists often differ on these attributions to the sephiroth. All any of us can do is use the attributions which "feel" right to us.

The *right* attribution is the one that seems instinctively so. For example, many decks of tarot cards, and every book on ceremonial magic (except one), and many other witches contend that the weapon for Air is the Sword, for Fire, the Wand. I, however, am an Air/Wand, Fire/Sword person and always have been. Fire *burns* a wand, and I can't feel that a weapon is appropriate if it can be destroyed by the element it is supposed to control. That's just my opinion, however. Even some members of my coven are Air/Sword folks, and that is their privilege. These things are too personal for others to judge.

The Archangel of this sphere is Gabriel. You may be familiar with him as the Archangel of Water, but he is known also in the Christian mythos as the archangel who will blow the trumpet announcing Judgment Day. The Qabala may be the indirect source of this legend, just as it may be the source of the "old man on a throne" picture of God.

Yesod is not only the last step before physical manifestation, but the first step after the end of manifestation as well. The image of Gabriel standing over graves from which people are rising may have filtered down from the idea of the spirit leaving its now useless physical body.

Gabriel and his angels, the Aishim, guide spirits, or souls if you prefer, into their physical bodies before birth, and away from them after death. They are "in charge" of arranging or designing the forms which manifest in Malkuth, the physical plane. The matter itself is in Malkuth, but the forces which hold it together and give it life are Yesodic forces.

Many authorities place the underworld and its deities in Yesod, while I've placed them in Binah. Yesod, the first step after physical death, is where we would find ourselves after we leave our bodies behind. But this death of the body is only one ending when we cease to be incarnate. During our time between lives, we must suffer the death of the personality, cease to be who we are in this life. I believe this to be a function of Binah.

Perhaps immediately after physical death, we do find ourselves in a type of underworld, one whose form is different for everyone: Heaven or Hell, the Summerland, the realm of Pluto. We would, immediately after death, be very much influenced by our present personalities and their thoughts, so here we would remain, temporarily, until we are ready to continue. I would probably find myself trembling in the Hall of the Assessors, with Osiris and the Eater of Hearts waiting for me.

The Vice of Yesod is Idleness. Teachers will recognize this. How often have students who first worked very hard in their studies suddenly refused to put forth any further effort? This often passes, of course, but if it does not, the students do not advance. They remain in the Treasurehouse of Images, bemused by what they see, accepting it as truth. They are convinced they have found it all and do not need to travel further. There is no further need for work or study. They know it all. Not for them the uphill climb, the soul-searching, the struggle to know their true Self, the striving for growth and change. They have flown to the top of the mountain, and see all, know all.

The Illusion of Yesod is Security, and that fits quite well with this attitude. In order to grow, you must change, and change is frightening. People at this stage believe they are secure; their foundation is firm. They have achieved everything that is needed, and none of that frightening change is necessary.

They are, of course, mistaken. Yesod is indeed the foundation, but not in the sense of a building's foundation. My dictionary defines *foundation* as "the basis on which something stands or is supported." The sea will support you, if you float on it, but the sea is also everchanging and moving. It is also the very foundation of life on this planet.

Think about this a minute. Those at this stage are "standing" on what they think is a rock-solid foundation. They are really standing on a raft in mid-ocean—and there are storms ahead.

What you must do to dispel this illusion, and overcome the Vice of Idleness is to trust, for Trust is the Obligation of

Yesod. Those so "secure" in their own knowledge (which we have seen is no knowledge at all) think that they do not need to trust anyone. Now that they know it all, they do not need to depend on anyone else. That means they don't ever have to trust anyone else. If not needing to trust someone else makes you feel secure, doesn't that imply a fear of trusting?

You can't live that way, you know. You can't *grow* that way. There are many times in life when you *must* take chances, must make a leap of faith, must trust in someone or something.

The truly sad part is that these people believe they have achieved the Virtue of Yesod, which is Independence, but independence means something more than not depending on anyone else. It means "self-governing." You govern yourself. You control yourself, discipline yourself, rule yourself. But, in order to govern yourself, you must come to know yourself. Your *Self.* That does not happen in a day. It rarely happens without work.

Work? Eeek!

I know. You don't need to work. You've got it all already.

Wrong, bright eyes! You're just beginning. Trust me. There's that word again. Why is it so necessary?

Sometime in the future, there are experiences coming that are necessary for your spiritual growth. These experiences, as I've said before, are some of the most difficult you will ever go through, and ones from which you will learn more than you can imagine.

You will learn things about yourself you have refused to see. Some of these will be your strengths, but many will be your weaknesses, the areas you need to change. These weaknesses will be brought home to you in ways that will force you to see them. You will not be able to escape.

That will you do when you discover that this Self in whom you have placed all your trust has faults, isn't perfect? If this is the foundation on which you stand, you are going to find yourself standing in midair — no rock, no raft, no nothing. Think about it.

If, however, your foundation is built on trust—in the gods, in the wisdom of your teachers, in the fact that you know there is much to learn, in the knowledge that even this experience is part of the natural order, and that you will not only survive it, but be glad it happened—you will spare yourself a great deal of pain and fear.

It is to be hoped that the powers of Yesod continue to flow into those who succomb to the Illusion of Security and bring forth the Virtue of Yesod, Independence.

One difference between Eastern and Western philosophies is the difference in the relationship between teacher and student. In an effort to escape from Self, an Eastern student is taught total blind obedience to the teacher. Within this philosophy is a valid teaching — you become one with all and begin by ceasing to think of the ego, the singular self.

In Western traditions, however, students are trained to learn within their own minds, to seek the deity within, recognize it, grow toward it. Life is not avoided; it is sought out for the lessons it has to teach. One reaches for the deity within. One conquers everyday life, instead of avoiding it. Independence, therefore, is a most desirable quality in a student. Questions, doubts, ideas, and thoughts *should* flow into the mind of a student.

This time becomes a test for the teacher. In a sense, teachers are parents, and it is often difficult for parents to allow children to grow up. They feel a pang of loss when children begin to think for themselves, develop minds of their own. Parents must let go, let children make their own decisions and their own mistakes.

So often when a student and teacher first come together, the student hungers for knowledge, sits at the feet of the teacher, if only symbolically, and soaks in every word, every thought, every instruction. Teachers are human beings, and this is a wonderful feeling, this feeling of power. If we teachers have grown as we should have, we will allow our students to grow, to become adults in the Craft. We will give up the ego boost of having students hang on our every word, depend on us for every spiritual thought.

We're human, we'll feel the pain of losing that adulation, but it can be replaced by a feeling of pride as our students move forward, upward, grow, perhaps even surpass us in knowledge.

It can be a joy, too, to observe the results of the Yesod Spiritual Experience, the "Vision of the Machinery of the Universe." I consider this one of the most strengthening, most comforting of all the experiences. This vision does not mean that students will understand totally the divine plan, the holy workings of the Universe, but students who have had this experience know that there is a plan, that the machinery exists. That cry of "Why?" into the darkness I spoke of in an earlier chapter is, in a sense, answered by this experience. You may not know why, but you will know there is a reason; you will know that of a certainty. You will know that things will be as they should, and that you will understand. You become aware that the Wheel of Life is *rolling*, not spinning. You will still experience the ups and downs of the Wheel, but you will know that every time you reach the bottom, you are further ahead than the last time; you are moving forward. Small trials become almost unimportant; large ones you will analyze for the lessons they contain.

Several characters in the novel, *Green Light*, by Lloyd C. Douglas have this experience.[2] One of the characters says that he knows he is part of the Divine Plan, that delays are only red lights, and that when it is time for him to move forward, he'll see the green light. The awareness that gives such comfort and, yes, even joy, to the people in this book can be none other than the Vision of the Machinery of the Universe.

How wonderful to know, in the depth of yourself, that we are all moving forward, together, as one. This is the greatest teaching of Yesod. Once *truly* felt, truly experienced, the Vice of Idleness must disappear, for you are carried forward by the wave of humanity struggling toward its source. Through the coming dark nights of the soul, that Vision can sustain you.

---

[2] Lloyd C. Douglas, *Green Light* (New York: Grosset & Dunlap, 1935).

The Magical Image that will help you contact all that Yesod represents is a beautiful naked man, very strong. He represents the potential, the fertility of the sphere. A young fertile woman would not be inappropriate, but in the male figure, the potential for fertility is physically obvious. Use of the male figure also prevents any confusion with the Magical Image of the Netzach. The potential expressed by this image becomes what we call reality in Malkuth.

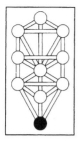

12

I AM
THE BEAUTY OF
THE GREEN EARTH

Before heaven and earth had taken form, all was vague and amorphous. Therefore it was called the Great Beginning. The Great Beginning produced emptiness and emptiness produced the universe. . . . The combined essences of heaven and earth became the yin and yang, the concentrated essences of the yin and yang became the four seasons, and the scattered essences of the four seasons became the myriad creatures of the world.

—Huai-nan Tzu[1]

BEFORE WE DISCUSS this sphere, I'd like to take a moment to discuss briefly the path between Yesod and Malkuth, the "32nd Path."

One of the symbols of this path is Saturn, the Planetary Attribution of Binah, the idea of form. It is most appropriate to find a reflection of Binah on the path approaching physical manifestation, concrete form.

The color of this path is black. Many people who have "died" and been revived have reported the sensation of traveling through a dark tunnel. This fits perfectly with the symbology of traveling from the sphere of Malkuth, the physical world, to Yesod, by way of the 32nd Path.

---

[1] Huai-nan Tzu, *Treatise*, in *Butler's Familiar Quotations* (Boston: Little Brown, 16th edition, 1992), p. 86.

We travel this path from Yesod to Malkuth, a world we have little difficulty understanding, the physical world, the world of manifestation. Malkuth means "The Kingdom." Its planet is, of course, the Earth, but Malkuth contains all that is physical and therefore, the solar systems, planets, and galaxies. Be careful here to avoid any confusion of your "earths." There is the planet Earth, the element of Earth, and the sphere of Malkuth, which includes both of the others.

The deities of Malkuth are all Earth deities, corn or grain deities: Pan, Geb, Persephone, Ceres, etc.

Malkuth receives all the emanations of the other spheres; all the ideas, the potentialities, come together in its "reality." For many, this is the only reality.

All spheres are equally holy, equally divine. We must not make the mistake of considering Malkuth a lesser sphere than the others. It is as vital a part of the Tree as Kether is. One analogy for the place of Malkuth on the Tree is to consider a light bulb. The electricity flows down one wire through the light bulb, producing light, then back through another wire to its source, just as the energy of Kether flows through the spheres to Malkuth, is made manifest, and completes the circuit by returning to Kether.

It is said that the Tree is upside down, having its roots in Heaven. This means that Malkuth is the top of the Tree, not its bottom. A text from the *Sepher Yetzirah* reads:

> The Tenth Path is the Resplendent Intelligence, because it is exalted above every head, and sits upon the Throne of *Binah*.[2]

This not only establishes Malkuth as the Top of the Tree, but expresses the presence of the Goddess in the physical world, and therefore its Divinity.

The refusal of many faiths to recognize the divinity in physical matter is the cause of most of the pathology, spiritual and

---

[2] W. Wynn Westcott, *Sepher Yetzirah* (New York: Samuel Weiser, 1975), p. 29.

emotional, encountered today. "As above, so below." If Kether is holy, so then is Malkuth. If Malkuth is not holy, neither is Kether, and that is ridiculous. The physical world is not a corrupt creation, separate from its Maker who is now embarrassed by His or Her creation. We and all that surrounds us, are an integral living part of our Lord and Lady, a vital part without which They would be incomplete.

Kether's Magical Image is a king. Malkuth's is a young queen, crowned and throned (or veiled, in some books). Crowned and throned . . . crowned and throned . . . the Crown of Kether and the Throne of Binah.

Kether is said to be entirely positive and Malkuth totally feminine, receptive to all other spheres. We come down the Tree from pre-being to physical being. Now, whether we are using this glyph or not, we are working back up the Tree to Kether, having learned and grown and become something more than we were through our experiences. We reach from this physical life to that which is our source. That reaching, that going forth is positive, so Malkuth is also masculine, or positive.

One of Malkuth's titles is the "Gate of Death," a little confusing because we enter Malkuth when we are born. However, we leave it when our body dies and we cease, temporarily, to have a physical existence. In that sense, it is the Gate of Death, but the term is also appropriate in another sense.

Before entrance into Malkuth, we are not incarnate, not bound by physical being. At birth as we know it, we leave behind all that we know, start again with minds apparently bare of any knowledge. All we meet in Malkuth are strangers to us; we remember nothing of lives before or loved ones. Could this not be considered a form of death? Passing through this gate in either direction is both death and birth. At the death of the body, we rejoin our Great Selves, recover our memories, our knowledge; rejoin those we have known and loved. Death becomes birth.

The Archangel of Malkuth is Sandalphon, the Approacher, and his angels are the Kerubim, the Strong. In ceremonial magic, and in my Craft tradition, we deal with four other archangels in

Malkuth, the Archangels of the Elements. They, too, have angels over which they rule—divisions of the Kerubim. The angels do not have names as such, but are represented by the symbols of the fixed signs of the Zodiac. Raphael is the Archangel of Air, and his angels are the ♒. Michael is the Archangel of Fire; his angels, the ♌. Gabriel rules Water and the angels are signified by ♏. Over Earth is the Archangel Auriel, and his angels, the ♉.

When these symbols are used to signify the angels, they (the symbols) are called "kerubs." This is one of the reasons I place the Kerubim in Malkuth rather than Yesod. Another reason relates to the Old Testament, which, although not sacred to me as it is to Christians, is still interesting from a Qabalistic point of view. I am told that in some translations, the Old Testament states that when Adam and Eve were driven from Eden, a kerub bearing a fiery sword was placed "at the Gate" to prevent their return (Genesis 3). While I have been unable to find this version, I mention it because Malkuth has no less than three titles which refer to it as a Gate. The attribution of the Kerubim therefore seems very fitting, very natural, and very right to me.

The Name of Power of Malkuth is Adonai Ha Aretz, "Lord of Earth." Again, the translation is masculine, and inappropriate if Malkuth is entirely feminine. It will work just as well with Adonath, "Lady of Earth." If we are working up the Tree, in meditation for example, Lord of Earth is appropriate.

The Vice of Malkuth is Inertia—the principle that an object at rest tends to remain at rest. The Great Work, the way which holds that we can shorten our time on the Wheel of Life by deliberate growth, is a difficult one, and the first step is the most difficult. Many are reluctant to take it. A part of us, probably not a conscious part, knows the pain and effort and frustration involved in the Work, and fights against taking that first irretrievable step.

The Illusion of Malkuth is Materialism, and indeed those beginning on a spiritual path often do feel that having the right tools and the right book and the right robe is extremely important. Concentration on collecting these items uses up a lot of time and energy and makes it possible to ignore the fact that you aren't going anywhere.

The Obligation of this sphere is Discipline, the obvious quality needed to break the Inertia which keeps you from moving forward. Only with discipline can you take the steps you need to go forward, something the Vice is trying to prevent you from doing.

Once you have known the Vision of the Holy Guardian Angel, you know that you must go forward through all the dark nights ahead, and this Vision is the Spiritual Experience of Malkuth. This Holy Guardian Angel is your Inner Self, your Greater Self, that of which you, in your present personality, are a part. This is the "bright being" radiating love seen by so many who have been clinically dead and returned to life.

This is the you that is aware of all your lives, all your pasts, your lessons (learned and unlearned), your trials, your successes, your failures; your own Tree of Life of which you are a branch; the real you, the eternal you, the most holy, divine part of you. The vision teaches that there is more than the personality in which you are manifest.

The simplest way to express this is a belief in reincarnation. Now is not all there is, not your only life. You have had, will have, others. With this knowledge comes the understanding that there must be a reason for many lives, and eventually, the knowledge that this reason must be growth.

We know that growing up is difficult. "Growing pains" are very real. We can all look back in this life to the hurtful times, the despairing times, the agonizing times, and realize that we have become adults because of them. Imagine how much greater is the pain involved in the growing of the spirit. All of us will grow, will return to our Source; it cannot be avoided. But some of us know that by deliberate work we can shorten the time of this growing, and we have chosen the shorter and more arduous path. Once that decision is made and the first step taken, we cannot turn back even if we try. It takes effort and determination to make that first step. The second step is difficult, too, and since we cannot turn back, we slow down.

There is something in us that fears the pain to come, and it will help us find any excuse not to do the work we need to do. Eventually, however, we do make another step forward. Once that step is taken, another problem arises. We can be confused by the many paths that lead forward, or seem to. When we search and choose the right one (and there is a different one for each person), we've developed the Virtue of Malkuth, Discrimination.

The Briatic Correspondence of Malkuth is Stability, and you'll realize the value of that stability once you've realized that you do not, if you wish to grow, remain in Malkuth; you stand on it.

In your list of correspondences, you'll find that the Perfume for Malkuth is Dittany of Crete. Dittany, when used as an incense, produces not only a distinctive odor, but also a tremendous amount of smoke. Again, on your list of correspondences, you'll see that the Magical Weapons of this sphere are the Magical Circle and the Triangle of Art. In ceremonial magic, the Magical Circle is a protective one and the Triangle of Art is used to contain demons or whatever spirit is conjured up. In order to maintain a physical manifestation, the entity must have some physical material from which to create a form. The smoke of Dittany provides that.

I doubt that you wish to conjure up any demons, but this bit of information can give you an inkling as to how certain attributions were made. Whatever the original reasons behind them, they have taken on greater power through constant use, and their meaning has grown.

"Playing" with the attributions of the Qabala is an excellent way to learn and absorb it. Search for Qabalistic symbolism around you. You might gain from playing a bit with the few Hebrew words you've learned so far. The comment on the "wheels" of Ezekiel is one example (see page 42). Another is taking the sentence "Unless ye become as a little child, ye cannot enter the kingdom . . . " and substituting "Malkuth" for

"Kingdom." It means something entirely different that way, doesn't it?

Think on the myths of the pantheon you work with. Can you find anything there that fits on the Tree? What of the various deities you worship? In what spheres would you place them?

We have reached the bottom (or top) of our Tree. The following chapters will provide further information on how to put it to use.

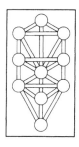

13

THE FOUR WORLDS

Four be the things I am wiser to know . . .
—Dorothy Parker[1]

EACH SPHERE, and indeed the Tree itself, is divided into four levels, or worlds, symbolized by the Flashing Colors; one color, or combination of colors, for each world. In Hebrew, these four worlds are:

Atziluth—the Archtypal World

Briah—The World of Creation (from the Hebrew for "giving shape."

Yetzirah—The World of Formation (from the Hebrew for "forming."

Assiah—The World of Manifestation (from the Hebrew for "completing."

These worlds each represent a level or type of energy as it manifests in the spheres. I prefer the following terms for these energies:

Atziluth—Deity Force
Briah—Archangel Force

---

[1] Dorothy Parker, *The Poems & Short Stories of Dorothy Parker* (New York: Random House, 1994), p. 53.

Yetzirah—Angelic Force
Assiah—Planetary or Elemental Force

The Deity Force represents the creative urge. The Archangel Force represents the creation of a concept. The Angelic Force produces the image, and the Planetary Forces are the final manifestation.

The World of Assiah, often called the mundane chakras, includes the powers symbolized by the planets and the circle of the zodiac. The "planetary" world in Malkuth is manifest in the four mystic elements.

These four worlds can be equated to the spiritual meaning of the quarterly sabbats:

Deity Force—Winter
It is at this season that the Sun is born. Although it is not obvious on the Solstice, the "direction" of the Sun has changed. To use the agricultural analogy, at this time of year, we consider and choose what we wish to grow in the year to come. Key phrase: The seed is chosen.

Archangel Force—Spring
At this season, when the Earth bursts into life, we plant that which we wish to grow. Key phrase: The seed is planted.

Angelic Force—Summer
In the Summer, that which we have planted has (we hope) sprouted and grown and, although its growth is not complete, we can see the form it will take. Key phrase: That which was planted takes form.

Planetary Force—Autumn
It is at this season that the growth is completed, and we harvest that which we have planted and grown, that which we have earned. What was begun in Winter is manifest in Autumn. Key phrase: The seed is gathered.

Yet another way to view the flow of energy from one world to another, from creative urge to manifestation, is as a journey.

Deity Force: The direction is chosen.
Archangel Force: The first step is taken, the journey begun.
Angelic Force: The journey continues.
Planetary Force: The destination is reached.

The Deity Force says: "There should be a way to clean up that dirt." The Archangel Force says: "The best way would be to have something suck it up." The Angelic Force produces the design. The Planetary Force produces a vacuum cleaner.

The Deity Force says: "Millions of televisions and with only one use. That's such a waste of knowledge and technology." The Archangel Force says: "Well, we'll just have to figure out another way to use them." The Angelic Force goes to work on it and the Planetary Force produces Pac-Man.

I thought: "Too bad so many pagans don't know how wonderful Qabala is." Then I thought, "I should tell them." My next thought was, "I could write a book."

VOILA!

• • •

This is admittedly a brief overview of this aspect of Qabala. If it intrigues you, I recommend *Ladder of Lights* by W. G. Gray in which each sphere, and the Four Worlds within are explored in detail.

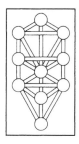

14

THE PATHS

So many gods, so many creeds, so many paths that wind and wind.

—Ella Wheeler Wilcox[1]

WHILE IT ISN'T PRACTICAL to do an in-depth discussion of the paths in this book, I would like to touch on them briefly.

There are 22 paths joining the spheres to each other. Obviously, there could have been more, but this is the number decided on ages ago. (See figure 21, page 33.)

The paths themselves are numbered 11 through 32. Why? Because the spheres are considered the first ten paths. Why? I don't know.

The paths signify the transition from one sphere to another. Therefore, the spheres are states of being, and the paths states of becoming. They have their own sets of correspondences, their own file folders, their own subdirectories.

To begin to understand the paths, first get as much understanding as you can of the spheres. Then try to consider what the transition between the spheres signifies. What is happening when Kether, the idea of being, is becoming Chokmah, the idea of force? This is the 11th path, traveling down. On the return trip, however, the idea of force is becoming the idea of being. What does that mean? What is happening then?

---

[1] Ella Wheeler Wilcox, "The World's Need," in *The Oxford Dictionary of Quotations* (London: Oxford University Press, 1985), p. 72.

It is in this way that you will learn the most about the paths. Below are some brief notes that might help you, and some questions to consider. The paths are not listed in numerical order, but rather in groups that have some connection.

11th Path (Kether to Chokmah)—The idea of being becoming the idea of force.

12th Path (Kether to Binah)—The idea of being becoming the idea of form.

The two energies necessary for creation come to be. The God and Goddess are born.

14th Path (Binah to Chokmah)—The idea of force and the idea of form come together to create being.

Remember I said that between Chokmah and Binah was the Great Rite? This is where that happens. Consider all I said about thinking of the two spheres together.

13th Path (Kether to Tifareth)—The unknowable becomes the knowable.

15th Path (Chokmah to Tifareth)—Pure force flows to the center of the Tree to be balanced with pure form.

17th Path (Binah to Tifareth)—Pure form flows to the center of the Tree to be balanced with pure force.

These three paths come together in Tifareth, the center of the Tree, the first point of balance on the Tree since Kether. Each of these paths crosses at least one horizontal path, and therefore signifies a Dark Night of the Soul, those times when you must go through pain and despair in order to learn and grow.

16th Path (Chokmah to Chesed)—The absolute masculine descending toward the Sphere of Expansion.

18th Path (Binah to Geburah)—The absolute feminine descending to the Sphere of Restriction.

Chesed and Geburah are the first spheres to contain both masculine and feminine elements. Although there are no paths between Binah and Chesed, or Chokmah and Geburah, yet those energies exist in those spheres. Binah and Chokmah have touched each other on the 14th path, and each sends the results down these two paths.

19th Path (Chesed to Geburah)—A balance of mercy and severity. Again, consider each sphere in light of the other, and then consider the significance of this path.

20th Path (Chesed to Tifareth)—The energy of the Masculine Pillar flows to the center.

22nd Path (Geburah to Tifareth)—The energy of the Feminine Pillar flows to the center.

The qualities of each of these spheres are sent to the center of the Tree. Each of the five spheres that have paths to Tifareth brings something different. How is the energy from Geburah different from that which comes from Binah? How is the energy of Chesed different from that which comes from Chesed? Contemplation of these questions will tell you more about these two paths.

24th Path (Tifareth to Netzach)—Energy again divides and flows to the Pillar of Expansion.

26th Path (Tifareth to Hod)—Energy again divides and flows to the Pillar of Restriction.

All that has come together in Tifareth is again divided and sent out to these two spheres. Knowing what you know about Hod and Netzach, in what ways does the energy of these paths differ?

25th Path (Tifareth to Yesod)—You can see that this path crosses the 27th, another horizontal path. Therefore it does signify another Dark Night of the Soul, one of the earliest in your spiritual growth. Yet Tifareth is named Beauty, Harmony. How do you suppose the energy from such a lovely sphere, such a spiritually significant sphere could represent something so difficult?

27th Path (Hod to Netzach)—The first horizontal path coming up the Tree. The balance between the two pillars on yet another level. The balance between thought and instinct, between force and form on a level you can understand.

30th Path (Hod to Yesod)—The Sphere of the Mind to the Sphere of Thoughtforms.

28th Path (Netzach to Yesod)—The Sphere of Creative Energy to the Sphere of Thoughtforms.

With the 25th Path, these paths join in Yesod, the last sphere before physical manifestation. Consider what the three spheres represent, and what they would be sending to this sphere.

31st Path (Hod to Malkuth)—Logic and order flow to the Physical Realm.

29th Path (Netzach to Malkuth)—Creative energy flows to the Physical Realm.

32nd Path (Yesod to Malkuth)—Balance and harmony flow to the Physical Realm.

The energies of the three pillars come together in physical manifestation.

The Major Arcana of the tarot can be useful in meditating on the paths. See chapter 16 for further information on that subject.

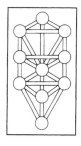

15

CREATING YOUR OWN TREE

*But each for the joy of working, and each, in his separate
star, shall draw the thing as he sees it . . .*
—Rudyard Kipling[1]

BEFORE YOU DO ANY real work with the Tree of Life, I
suggest you create your own personal Tree. Having it in easy
sight as you study and/or meditate will facilitate your learning
and absorption of the Qabala. My own Tree is before me now,
as it has always been as I was writing.

I encourage you to make a big production out of the creation of your own Tree. Make the drawing and coloring a ritual. If this Tree is to be used by a group, the group should
participate; each participant adding color to each sphere, discussing its meaning, vibrating the Name of Power, and whatever else will make the ritual meaningful.

If the Tree is for personal use, make it a private ritual, pondering the spheres as you apply the color, vibrating the deity
name, etc.

The effects of the ritual, and the resulting Tree, will be en-
hanced if you use a medium in which colors can be mixed,
rather than crayons or felt-tip pens. Use the clearest, cleanest,
brightest colors you can find. As we discussed in chapter 13 on
the Four Worlds, use the archangel colors. The colors for each

---

[1] Rudyard Kipling, "When Earth's Last Picture," in *The Oxford Dictionary of
Quotations* (London: Oxford University Press, 1983), p. 304.

of the Four Worlds are referred to as scales, i.e., Deity Scale, Archangel Scale, and so forth. The paths, if you paint them, are done in the deity colors.

Did somebody say why? Look at another way of expressing the color scales of the Four Worlds:

Deity—King Scale
Archangel—Queen Scale
Angelic—Prince Scale
Planetary—Princess Scale

Note that the deity and angelic scales are represented by masculine figures (force), the archangel and planetary scales by feminine ones (form). The spheres are states of being and are therefore static, unchanging. The paths are states of becoming and are therefore moving and changing, active. Therefore, use a negative or form color for the spheres, and a positive or force color for the paths.

Kether's archangel color is "Pure white brilliance." Granted, it is difficult to find a paint to express "brilliance," so use the whitest white available, perhaps zinc white. This will serve even better if your background is not quite white; a cream or off-white will make the sphere stand out even more.

All colors are included in white light. All that is to come, that is to be, all the significance of the other colors are within white. Whatever paint you use, it will only be a poor approximation of Kether's true meaning, but your very consideration of this as you color the sphere will be important.

Chockmah is a clean, cloud-like gray . . . clouds forming out of the invisible water vapor in the sky, becoming visible.

Binah is black, preferably a flat or matte black. Black is the absence of all color. No rays are returned; nothing is bounced back. Black receives all, as Binah is the epitome of receptivity.

Use a pure blue for Chesed, an equally clear red for Geburah, and a golden, gleaming, sun-yellow for Tifareth.

Move from the primary colors to those which must be mixed. Emerald green is the proper color for Netzach, pure blue and pure yellow. As you mix, striving for the color you desire, consider the significance of the two colors and the meaning of the mixture. Hod is orange, a combination of red and yellow. Yesod is violet, the blending of pure red and pure blue.

Now to Malkuth, whose colors are usually given as citrine, russet, olive, and black. I had some difficulty understanding the use of these colors until I talked with an artist whose knowledge of mixing colors clarified it for me. Olive is created by mixing red and green; russet by mixing orange and blue. AHA!

Then comes black, the same color as Binah. Remember that Malkuth sits upon the throne of Binah, and the color at the base of Malkuth is black. There is a difference, however. In Binah, you are dealing with light, and there black absorbs all rays. In Malkuth, however, you are dealing with the physical world, with paint, and therefore with the presence of all colors. If you use a glossy paint here, you will differentiate easily between the two aspects of black.

Citrine is not so easily dealt with, and it is with the deepest respect and apologies to Dr. Regardie, Ms. Fortune, Mr. Gray, Mr. Butler, Mr. Knight, and Mr. Crowley that I submit the following: Citrine doesn't work.

Olive is a mixture of the three primary colors, with blue predominating; russet, a mixture of the three with red predominating. It follows that the quarter expressed as citrine should be a mixture of the three with yellow predominating. But citrine is "lemon-yellow," achieved by adding a touch of blue to yellow. There is no red. The color for this quarter, the result I get when I actually *mix* the colors is ochre, a mixture of purple and yellow.

I can think of four possible explanations for the attibution of citrine.

1. A mistranslation somewhere along the line. A scholar of the Hebrew language might know of a word for "lemon-yellow" and a word for a shade of "yellow-brown" that are similar.

2. Lemons were, once upon a time, a very different color.

3. A reader has told me about another citrus fruit called a citron. She had seen them in the Middle East and they were more

of an ochre than a citrine. My encyclopedia says they are green-ish-yellow, so I don't know; but the possibility remains that the words citron and citrine were accidently switched.

4. It's one of those cute little curves the writers of old used to confuse the uninitiated.

In every other correspondence, I agree with at least one of the experts, but in this one I must differ. The choice, as always, is yours.

Don't, by the way, feel restricted to drawing and painting. I embroidered a very beautiful Tree on a natural muslin background. Another way is to create a relief plaque. Styrofoam balls, cut in half, sealed with a water-base spackle, can be painted and glued to a background. The paths can be wire, or dowels cut in half.

A very effective tree can be created with styrofoam balls or ping-pong balls put together like Tinker Toys. (For that matter, you could use Tinker Toys, but you'd have a flat disk instead of a sphere.) If the paths of the Middle Pillar are made from one strong piece of wire that extends beyond Malkuth, the wire could be inserted into a base. Alternatively, the wire could extend past Kether, be bent into a loop, and your tree could be hung from the ceiling.

There's one idea I've always wanted to try, but it would have to be big. I've always wanted to do a collage of the Tree with each sphere a separate collage of pictures of the correspondences—the Magical Image, the animal, the deities, and so forth. Wouldn't that be fabulous?

Be creative. You might find an entirely new way to depict the Tree.

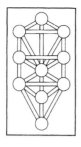

16

THOU WHO THINKEST
TO SEEK ME

To strive, to seek, to find . . .
—Alfred Lord Tennyson[1]

YOU HAVE YOUR OWN Tree of Life before you and are ready to do some work with this wonderful tool. How do you use it? In a hundred, a thousand ways, my friend, but I can share only a few.

THE QABALISTIC CROSS

This simple exercise should be the first thing you memorize. It is a good way to prepare for ritual and meditation, or simply to clear away negativity and get grounded. I've used it as a minor protective rite to keep away negativity sent by others.

Stand quietly for a moment, breathing deeply and rhythmically, and still your thoughts.

Imagine you are growing larger and larger with each breath. Your head touches the ceiling, passes through it. You are now looking down at the roof, at all the roofs in your neighborhood.

Now the city is stretched out before you; the state, the continent.

---

[1] Alfred, Lord Tennyson, "Ulysses," I:44 in *The Oxford Dictionary of Quotations* (London: Oxford University Press, 1955), p. 541.

The spinning Earth is below you, tiny and growing tinier.

You are larger than the solar system, the galaxy, all of creation. You stand in total darkness.

Imagine that out of the darkness a brilliant beam of light comes and forms a brilliant swirling sphere of light just above your head. Don't force it. Let it be there.

Vibrate the word "Atoh" (or "Ateh" if you prefer Ashkenazic Hebrew) as you touch your forehead. A beam of light comes from the sphere to your forehead as you touch it.

Picture the beam of light flowing through your body down to your feet as you point to them and vibrate "Malkuth." The light forms there another sphere, half above and half below ground level.

Touch your right shoulder and visualize another sphere of light forming there as you vibrate "Ve Geburah."

Draw your hand across your chest and touch your left shoulder vibrating "Ve Gedulah," as a fourth sphere of light forms on your shoulder.

You now have a cross of light extending from your head to your feet and from your right shoulder to your left.

Clasp your hands at the intersection of the cross. Vibrate "Le Olahm," as a fifth sphere of light forms around your hands. This sphere of light continues to expand until it fills your entire aura.

Stand a moment in this light and vibrate "Amen."

A version that is a bit more pagan is the following. It has not been used enough to build up the power that the original has, but it has a nice effect.

Directing your words to the Lord and Lady, visualize the sphere above your head, touch your forehead and say:

> Thou art
> The Kingdom (point to feet),
> The Strength (touch right shoulder),
> The Mercy (touch left shoulder),
> And the Love (clasp hands),
> Forever (sphere of light expands).
> So mote it be."

What you've done here is to place yourself in an energy circuit from, you could say, "Heaven to Earth." You'll find this healing, steadying, and, as I said, grounding.

I remember a time when, due to stress, I was really frazzled. I was ready to give up writing, teaching—everything. A young High Priest I know happened to drop by to pick up some papers I'd promised him. He asked if I'd demonstrate the Qabalistic Cross for him. I ran through the words and motions quickly. He then expressed a desire to see me perform it as I would in ritual. I did. As I stood there in the sphere of light, he said, "How do you feel?"

"Quiet," I said. "More grounded. Stable."

"Then why don't you do it more often?"

Don't you just hate smart alecks?

MEDITATION

Meditation is one of the most important tools for growth that exists. Whether you have a teacher or are studying alone, I don't think you can accomplish much without meditation. The changes that need to take place within you are often subtle, and the use of this particular tool can bring on those changes on many levels, many of which you will be unaware, at least for a time.

Two important things about meditation: First, the results do not always show at the moment. The changes often take place gradually, and you won't realize they are happening until later. Don't be discouraged if you don't seem to have results of a meditation right after it is finished.

Second, to get the most out of your meditations, it is important to write down what results you do have. Do this every time. I cannot stress too much how important this is. It will be one way for you to be aware of your growth, especially (but not limited to these times) when you repeat a meditation.

Do repeat them. Don't feel that once around each meditation subject is enough. Do each many times.

Before discussing the various Qabalistic meditations, it might be worthwhile to discuss the two types of meditation. It has been my experience that students are aware of only one type, passive meditation. This is the most common type, and benefits both spirit and body. Concentration on a focal point— a candle, a mandala, or a mantra—to the extent that all else is "blanked out" brings rest to the body and mind, and opens the spirit to the inflow of spiritual energies.

Active meditation is quite different. It might be called "concentrated contemplation." This is used to meditate "on" something. You should begin your meditation with the passive type to still your mind and narrow your concentration. Then you move on to your active phase.

If, for example, you are meditating on one of the Magical Images, perhaps "a young queen, crowned and throned," begin by visualizing this as clearly as possible. When the visualization is as complete as you can make it, see what thoughts, what questions come to you.

"Walk around" the image, look at it from all angles. What do you feel when you look at it? Follow each train of thought to see where it leads you. If your mind wanders too far afield, lead it gently back by vibrating the Name of Power of the sphere and/or going carefully over the image detail by detail.

If the image should begin to change, watch. After a bit, if this seems to be a matter of lessened concentration rather than developing ideas, reaffirm your mental image.

If you can, it is effective to *become* the image, see through the eyes of the young queen. Think her thoughts.

Active meditation is not only a learning process, but an invocation of the energies represented by the subject of the meditation, and its effects can be far-reaching.

The Tree has many other subjects for meditation: the symbols of the spheres, the deities attributed to each, as well as the planets. You can contact the Archangels by imagining yourself surrounded by their colors, or as Gareth Knight suggests, picturing a pillar of energy, with the color swirling in it.

RISING ON THE PLANES

Another method of experiencing the Tree is known as "Rising on the Planes." There are several methods for doing this. Mine is as follows:

Imagine yourself surrounded by the planetary colors of Malkuth (black, rayed with yellow). The swirling colors change gradually to the angelic colors (ochre, russet, olive, and black, flecked with gold). The gold flecks disappear, leaving the archangel colors. After a while, your aura becomes pure yellow. Don't remain in this color too long—let the color change to citrine flecked with azure, the planetary colors of Yesod. These colors change gradually to purple, then violet, then indigo.

What you have done here with the use of color is to move from the Assiatic World of Malkuth to the Atziluth World of Yesod. If you wish to continue to another sphere, surround yourself with its planetary color and continue. When you have gone as high as you wish, drop back to the archangel color and remain there as long as you like. When you have completed your meditation, return by reversing your visualization.

ASTRAL TEMPLES

Another method for concentrating on a sphere is to build an astral temple for that sphere and do your meditation "there." Look at the list of correspondences in Appendix I (page 145) and use those symbols to design your temple. Build it by imagining your temple, building it in your mind. You can even "construct" it piece by piece. It will become a very real place when you've worked on it and in it long enough. You can combine this meditation with others, perhaps performing the other meditations in this temple.

Suggested descriptions of the temples of Malkuth, Yesod, Hod, and Netzach will be found in Appendix II (page 173). These are the descriptions I use; you may add to or change them if it suits you, as long as you keep the symbolism within the proper correspondences for the spheres.

MANTRAS

Mantras are somewhere between active and passive meditation, although a bit closer to passive. You combine rhythmic breathing with a phrase mentally repeated.

For example, if you wish to work with Yesod, to learn more about the sphere, or develop your divination skills:

Choose an eight-syllable phrase which relates to the sphere. In this case, use "Oh, Silver Moon, help me to see."

Begin by getting comfortable and relaxing. Start breathing in a gentle four-beat rhythm. In-2-3-4, out-2-3-4, in-2-3-4, out-2-3-4.

It won't take long for your body to take up this rhythm. This rhythmic breathing is very good for you and can be done any time, anywhere.

When this rhythm becomes natural, mentally accompany the breathing with the mantra:

> In 2 3 4 Out 2 3 4
> Oh Sil ver Moon help me to see.

This alone will work very well, but if you like you can add a visualization to the chant.

When this becomes easy for you to do without much concentration, add the visualization of inhaling the Yesod archangel color. With each inhalation you draw in whirling, swirling violet light. It enters your lungs, and you can feel the energy of that light being absorbed. As you continue to breathe, mentally chant and inhale the energy-filled light, you will feel the energy enter your bloodstream and begin to circulate through your body with the energy that is Yesod. Eventually your physical body and your aura will be full of this whirling, swirling, violet light.

When you are ready to end the meditation, continue the breathing; picture the violet light becoming absorbed into your physical body. Let the violet color fade, although the energy remains.

After a moment or two, cease your chant.

Sit quietly, still breathing rhythmically. If thoughts come to you, make notes on them.

The breathing and mental chanting can be done almost any time. I often use a chant when I'm walking or gardening.

MAGICAL WORK

The meditation methods detailed above can be incorporated into specific magical work. You may add your own circle casting, invocations, prayers, etc.

If your work pertains to a specific sphere, gather what you can of the proper correspondences. For example, if you wish to do an invocation of Thoth, the great teacher, you could cover your altar with an orange cloth, use orange candles, burn storax, use an opal in the rite, have a statue or picture of the deity you wish to contact. Since the God in this case is Thoth, a statue or a picture of an ibis will do as well.

Hod's number is eight. You can incorporate this into the ritual in the form of knocks, the number of candles, an invocation repeated eight times. Use your imagination to make the ritual truly yours. Use one of the meditation methods to contact the powers represented by Hod and proceed with your work.

QABALISTIC SPELL CASTING

The following is a method of spell casting developed in the coven where I received my training. It can be used for any kind of a spell. Yes, any kind, even one with an unethical purpose. Magic is not inherently good or bad. It is intention that makes it so. If you intend to use any of the methods I describe for evil purposes, just remember the Law of Three. In modern parlance, that's "What goes around, comes around."

—First, decide which sphere is the appropriate one for your work. Choose a candle in the archangel color of that sphere.
—Sit or stand, holding your candle, and fill your aura with the brilliant deity light of Kether. Quickly change it to the archangel color and dwell on that for a moment. Proceed to the angel color, then to the planetary color. (This is the reverse of the Rising on the Planes.)
—If the sphere in which your work is centered is above Tifareth, continue through the spheres in order, going from deity color to archangel color to angelic color to planetary color, proceeding to the deity color of the next sphere. If it is below Tifareth, it is best to go through Tifareth instead of taking a short cut. This will insure that you remain balanced. When you reach the sphere you wish to work with, pause briefly at the deity color and vibrate the Name of Power a few times. Try to emanate the adoration and love you feel for Deity in all forms.
—Change to the archangel color, greet the archangel, and ask his help. Speak of or concentrate on the goal of your spell. Continue down the Tree by the use of the colors.
—When you reach the archangel color of Yesod, (Yes, *do* go through Yesod) pause and form a picture of your goal, as clearly and strongly and with as much detail as you can.
—Continue through Malkuth and light your candle to signify the transference of your thought form to physical reality.

—Repeat each day as necessary, using the same candle. Let it burn a certain amount each day, and extinguish it with the thought that it continues to burn on other planes. As often as you can during the day, add energy to your thought form by picturing it again.

A special note: Hod is always reached through Chesed and vice versa. (Hod. . . "has no root . . . except in the hidden places of Gedulah".)[2] Therefore it is correct to go from Chesed through Tifareth to Hod instead of taking the long way around. For healing, it is permissible to go straight down the Middle Pillar, from Kether to Tifareth to Yesod to Malkuth.

THE TAROT AND THE TREE

Although the tarot was not applied to the Tree until comparatively recently (the last few centuries,) the two do fit together rather nicely. (See figure 22, page 120.)

The Major Arcana of the tarot has 22 cards, one for each path on the Tree. The Minor Arcana has four suits of 13 cards each, ace through ten and four court cards. One card of the Major Arcana is, of course, applied to each of the 22 paths. Which path they go on is a matter of opinion, and almost everyone has a different opinion.

For example, Crowley felt that the Star should not be attributed to the 28th path between Yesod and Netzach. He places the Emperor there and moves The Star to the path between Chokmah and Tifareth. Personally, I place a card called The Stars there. Most Qabalists will not agree with my placement of the Tower on the 25th path and Temperance on the 27th. Which attribution should you use? The one that seems right to you. Until you are more familiar with the subject, pick one that is already in use, mine or someone else's. In time, you'll settle on the one that works best for you.

---

[2] W. W. Westcott, *Sepher Yetzirah* (New York: Samuel Weiser, 1975), p. 29.

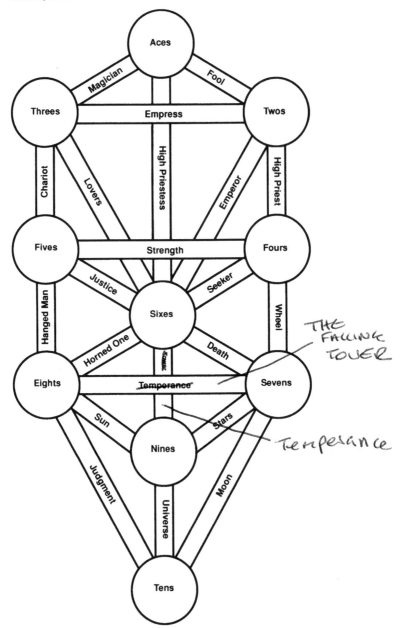

Figure 22.   The Tarot on the Tree.

The Minor Arcana are placed according to number: The aces are in Kether, the two's in Chokmah, the three's in Binah, and so forth.

The Court Cards are related to the Four Worlds in this manner:

Kings—Deity World
Queens—Archangel World
Princes or Knights—Angelic World
Princesses or Pages—Planetary World

Not all decks will work well with Qabala. If you want to incorporate tarot into your Qabalistic work (or Qabala into your tarot), you should choose one of the decks designed with that thought in mind. You are probably familiar with the Waite deck designed by A. E. Waite. It or any of the many decks incorporating Mr. Waite's designs will be excellent. Yet another approach is found in the Golden Dawn Tarot by Robert Wang and Israel Regardie, or the Golden Dawn Ritual Tarot by Chic and Tabi Cicero. These two decks have much in common with the Waite deck, but are in many ways quite different.

Naturally, for paganfolk, I would recommend my own deck, the Witches' Tarot. It includes both Qabalistic and pagan symbolism, and therefore might speak to many of you.

The Major Arcana have at least two uses in working with Qabala. They are excellent sources for meditation in themselves, representing as they do the paths on the Tree. Meditation on these cards will help you gain a greater understanding of the paths to which they are attributed.

You can also use them as doors to the paths between the spheres. Our tradition uses them in this way in various rituals given to signify a student's travels up the Tree.

If you wish to work with a sphere, and are doing so by imagining yourself inside it, place the cards around you to represent the paths leading out of the sphere.

All these methods of working with and using the Qabala can be used effectively on surface levels, but if you really want the Qabala to work for you, then you will have to work with it, and you start by memorizing as much as you can of the correspondences of the spheres. It is all very well to have a shelf full of reference books, but no list of correspondences, however complete, can accomplish what your own mind can do in correlating the information on different levels in different ways. Get that information into your memory on a permanent basis, and you will be surprised—nay, amazed at what comes out!

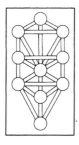

THE SOLITARY STUDENT

The life so short, the craft so long to learn.
—Hippocrates[1]

I WOULD NEVER SAY that an earthly teacher is an absolute necessity for spiritual growth, but it is certainly easier if you have one, and in many ways more effective. There is an ancient saying that when the student is ready, the teacher will appear. It is a true saying; one will eventually be made available to you if you are truly open to being taught.

The lack of a teacher is not an excuse for abandoning your search for spirituality. (The temptation to do so may be a symptom of the Vice of Malkuth, Inertia.) By all means, study, meditate, work, but be open to a teacher if the right one should come to you.

The biggest problem in studying alone is not lack of guidance or lack of answers to the questions you have, but lack of objectivity. To work alone successfully, you must concentrate on the extremely difficult and even painful development of a rare quality in humankind—the ability to look at yourself objectively, as if you were someone else. You must learn to view yourself honestly, to step aside and see yourself as others see you.

If you do not, you will not be aware of your reactions to the influx of energies of the various spheres as they occur. I've

---

[1] Hippocrates, *Aphorisms* I:i in *The Oxford Dictionary of Quotations* (London: Oxford University Press, 1983), p. 251.

mentioned one such reaction above, the Inertia of Malkuth. If you do not recognize it, you will not be able to push yourself out of it. One technique which might help you develop that detachment is to work on the development of your magical personality.

The first step in doing so is to choose a new name, a traditional step in many magical traditions. Your new name represents the "perfected" you—the person you are striving to become, the best part of your present self. This name should be chosen very carefully, and is not something to be rushed. In our coven, we have one requirement for such a name: It must have meaning for the person choosing it.

Some have chosen names of gods or goddesses, names that symbolize the qualities they are reaching for. Others have chosen the names of mythological characters they admire. In the past, members of the coven have chosen names from Tolkien. We discourage this, however. Not only are there too many people out there doing the same thing, but we want to prevent confusing fantasy fiction and magical reality. Some have created names that have meaning for them. The important thing is that the name be significant.

Take your time in making this choice. You can change the name later if you like (we all change as we grow and our names can reflect this), but the better suited your name is to you now, the more natural it feels, the more effective will be its use.

Once you've chosen such a name—let's say you've chosen George—start thinking of George as the mature you, and your everyday name, Harry, as the younger part. I'm not advocating the development of a split personality. Both names are you, but different views, different aspects of yourself. You can be Mommy or Daddy to your children, Son or Daughter to your parents, Harry or Harriet to your friends, and Pookie or Cuddlebumps to your beloved without being four different people. You can be George *and* Harry without becoming mentally disturbed.

Before you begin meditating, spell-casting, or performing a ritual of any kind, take a moment to "move in" to being George.

Leave behind jealousy, anger, fear, and any other type of negativity, bringing only the best of yourself into your circle. That's the first step.

The second is to practice seeing things from different points of view. Many of us do this often if we have developed any understanding of others at all. We can see things from another's standpoint, realize why they followed a certain course of action, understand and forgive. Some can even see, understand, and forgive when they themselves have suffered from another person's actions. I wish I could say I always do, but that would be untrue. I keep trying.

Spend some time trying to see things as others see them. If co-workers snap at you without apparent reason, try to understand why. Are they tired? Are they ill? Did someone else snap at them? Did *you* perchance get snippy first? Were you being irritating? Were they worried? Use your imagination and your intelligence.

Then apply that to yourself, being as objective as you can, by having George try to understand Harry. "Harry, why did you yell at so-and-so today?" If Harry's only reason was that he felt like it, that's a lousy reason and he needs some serious talking to.

If Harry answers, "Because so-and-so was right, and I didn't want to admit it, so I yelled," that's still a lousy reason, but an understandable one, a human one. So is "What she said hurt, and I didn't want her to know it."

George should congratulate Harry on his honest answer, and Harry should promise to do better. If Harry insists that his reasons were valid and he fully intends to do what he wants to, he hasn't learned a thing. However, if this were truly the case, Harry wouldn't be the kind of person who is trying to grow. Harry is still covering up that he's wrong, or hurt. Why on Earth (or any other plane) should Harry try to hide from himself? Because he's human, and if he admits he wasn't justified in his anger, his own opinion of himself will suffer.

Give yourself the same love, understanding, and forgiveness you would give anyone else, but don't let yourself get away with nonsense. If you never reveal your true, imperfect self to anyone else in the world, you must not hide it from yourself! In spiritual growth, it is imperative that you learn to be honest with yourself. If you do not admit faults, you will never work to change, and you will not grow, except in your ability to lie to yourself.

I've placed such an emphasis on this because, if you do not have a teacher to observe you, you will not be aware of your changes unless you have learned to observe and be truthful with yourself.

If you manage to break the Inertia of Malkuth, all well and good. After Malkuth comes Yesod, the Sphere of Illusion. Suddenly, it is all so clear! You can see beyond the horizon, know the future, solve everyone's problems. You don't have any problems. You are all-seeing, all-knowing, all-powerful. WOW! You can see everyone's faults (you don't have any of those either, having by some cosmic means attained instant perfection). Teacher? Who needs a teacher? You've got it all right at your fingertips. You could *be* a teacher. You're going to run right out and start a coven of your very own.

In other words, you are the magical equivalent of first-year psychology students who, having learned the terms and symptoms for psychological malfunctions, believe themselves immune to them.

When you reach this exalted state, become a semi-to-moderately instant adept, do yourself one small favor. Spend a few moments meditating on Joan Grant's interpretation of one of the questions asked by the 42 Assessors of Egyptian mythology:

Hast thou seen thy giant shadow on the wall and thought thy semblance mighty?[2]

I'm sure you can see the problems of studying without a teacher. They are not insurmountable, but your path can be a

[2] Joan Grant, *Winged Pharoah* (Columbus, OH: Ariel Press, 1985), p. 317.

very difficult, painful, and disheartening one without a teacher. Working *with* a teacher can be difficult, painful, and disheartening, too, but these things are easier to bear with the support and understanding of an experienced teacher.

What can you do without a teacher? Quite a bit. So far, I've mentioned many things which can be done alone, things which will be useful and helpful. If you are going to work with the Tree, using it as a structure for your own program, you'll find it very beneficial in deciding what to work on as you progress.

In chapter 18, I've listed information about the training program in Sothistar. You may find that, and other information in that chapter, useful. You don't have to follow the program exactly, but it might serve as a guideline toward your own studies. You might also pay attention to the stages students go through and the problems they might have, and keep an eye out for these problems as you travel your path.

I suggest that you set up a program for yourself, a schedule. Set a time for studies and for meditation. Decide what you want to concentrate on and stick to it. Do allow yourself some flexibility, but don't get too lax.

As you travel up the Tree, you'll find your goals changing. This isn't unexpected. Before you make any serious changes in your plans, give them careful consideration. (Give everything your careful consideration.) For example, you may find that your interest in one of the subjects you are studying leads you to further exploration of that subject and others related to it. That's fine, but don't neglect your other studies.

As you work with each sphere, try to understand what problems it presents for you, where your weaknesses are, and your strengths. When problems present themselves, pay close attention to see if there is a lesson to be learned from the problem. If there is, learn it. Don't seek out problems or difficult situations. Life will present them as you move along. Life can do a much better job of presenting lessons than you can.

Be hard on yourself, but not too hard. When you take a step forward, congratulate yourself. You probably won't recognize such a step until long after you take it, but congratulate yourself anyway.

Do keep a journal. Write down everything—your meditations, their results, the magical work you do, the books you've read and things in them that struck you as important. Don't be afraid to be truthful in your journal. No one will see it but you, and it can prove invaluable on your journey, especially when you read back to earlier entries. It will be a chronicle of your growth, and you'll be able to recognize the important stages, although you may not have been aware of them at the time.

However successful you may be alone, do remain open to a teacher should he or she come into your life. Work magically for that arrival.

If you decide to do a spell for a teacher using the form of spell casting contained in an earlier chapter, the sequence is Kether to Chokmah, to Binah, to Chesed, to Tifareth, to Hod, on to Yesod, and Malkuth. Use an orange candle, pause at Hod and vibrate the deity name, greet the archangel, etc. At Yesod, visualize yourself being taught, continue to Malkuth, and light your candle.

I urge you to make this attempt. And when you do find that you've been led to a teacher, use the Qabala to decide whether this is your teacher or you should keep looking.

In my opinion, a teacher should have had at the very least the Vision of the Machinery of the Universe, and preferably the Vision of Beauty Triumphant. Ideally, a teacher should have had both Tifareth experiences, but those are not always attained.

Having experienced these visions, a good teacher should have a basic optimism about life, a belief that there is a direction, a purpose. None of us are optimistic all the time, but a basic security in the workings of the Universe should be a prerequisite.

Take your time, as I'm sure the teacher will take his or hers. If you are not comfortable with the teacher or the group, and it seems to be a serious discomfort, look further. The first teacher is not always the right one for you.

Until you find *your* teacher, work alone and carefully. May the God and Goddess guide and bless you.

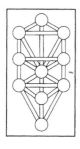

18

QABALA FOR TEACHERS AND GROUPS

And gladly would he learn and gladly teach.
— Geoffrey Chaucer[1]

AS A TEACHER, you have to be a scholar, psychologist, and spiritual advisor. You are expected to know all the answers, handle all problems, provide comfort and consolation. In addition to that, you must prepare classes, direct rituals and keep the group working together peacefully.

Qabala cannot solve all your problems, but it can make you a better teacher by helping you recognize, and even predict, the phases your students go through, as well as give you the proper techniques to guide your people through these phases.

The use of the Tree within my own tradition might suggest to you ways in which you can use it with your own students. My tradition has five "grades" which precede the First Degree. With the exception of the first one, Neophyte, each of these is related to a specific sphere on the Tree, and to a specific element.

During Neophyte, we teach "Sothistar 101," those things students need to know to function within our group—our circle casting, the techniques and meditations we use—so that they may attune themselves to the energies of the coven. Here

---

[1] Geoffrey Chaucer, *The Portable Chaucer*, Theodore Morrison, ed. (New York: Viking Press, 1975), p. 61.

we also teach the basics of the elements. Once these things have been learned, we begin the true journey up the Tree.

In Sothistar, elemental initiations begin with Earth, the sphere of Malkuth. "Initiation" here does not refer to First Degree where a student becomes an initiate. It refers to a ceremony that signifies the beginning of the student's work in an element or sphere. It should probably be called something else, but after 20 years, it's hard to change.

In Earth initiations, we invoke the element of Earth, so that during a student's time in this grade, the forces invoked bring forth problems which require work. In Earth grade, these are usually problems dealing with the physical plane: health, money, certain relationships, etc.

During the entire training program and beyond, teachers observe the students, pay attention to their growth, their advancement (or lack of it), and make a special effort to be aware of the student's reactions to the various forces brought into play.

For example, no matter how anxious students are to learn, how sincere, there comes a time in Earth grade when they cannot get going. It's difficult for them to concentrate on their studies; so many things are allowed to interfere. Inertia, the Vice of Malkuth, has set in. The First Law of Inertia states that an object at rest tends to remain at rest, so this is very difficult to overcome. We have learned to be patient, to keep encouraging students, and, if necessary, to administer a little kick to the other side of their laps (psychically speaking, of course) to get them moving again. The Second Law of Inertia states that an object in motion tends to remain in motion. Once they get started, they'll be fine.

The second step is Air grade, Yesod. (The Middle Pillar is the Air Pillar.) Again, the element invoked insures that the student will work on problems appropriate to the forces of Air, and the sphere of Yesod.

When students begin to work in Air, the vice of idleness sets in. It is at this point that many students fade away from the group, and often from the Craft altogether. They decide they've learned it all; we have nothing more to teach them; they have no further need of instruction from us. (See the discussion on Yesod's Vice page 86.) This may seem a strange way for idleness to manifest itself, but if students are instant adepts, have achieved instantaneous cosmic consciousness, they won't have to do all that horrible studying and hard work, will they? The Sphere of Illusion makes it easy for them to convince themselves.

Some of them will make it through this stage and continue up the Tree. Many won't. Let them go. They may return at a later time, embarrassed and repentant. Welcome them home, and move forward. If they don't return, your path was not theirs and your group is better off without them.

Whatever you do, don't blame yourself. It won't hurt to do some serious soul-searching to see if you could have done things differently, but, on the whole, this is the student's decision. Don't feel that accepting them as students was necessarily a mistake. It may be that they needed to spend some time with you (and you with them) and then move on.

One of my earliest students left shortly after achieving Air grade. He left after spending an evening telling me all the things I'd done wrong. I spent the entire night staring at the ceiling, going over and over what he'd said, wondering how much of it was right. It was one of my first really bad times as a teacher; it shook my faith in myself and my right to teach. Six years later, I received a letter from him, telling me that he finally understood the things I'd been trying to teach him.

There is a type of student who never makes it past Yesod. They go from group to group, giving the impression of a sincere desire to learn. What they really want is recognition of their incredible spiritual prowess, in the form of rapid advancement upward within the coven. When that is not forthcoming, they leave, fuming that they've "been at this for ten years and know more than the damned teacher."

Perhaps some day, they'll realize that those ten years mean nothing if they are spent bouncing up and down the 32nd path. You can spend ten years as a freshman and that will not earn you a B.A. Or, as a button I have proclaims, "Three first degrees do not equal a third."

The Qabala is not studied until Air grade in our tradition, although many Qabalistic techniques and references are used before then. You should see the "Aha!" expressions as students recognize the significance of a meditation or chant they've been using.

Water grade is Hod, and students' work here is accompanied first by the Vice, Dishonesty, and finally the Virtue, Truthfulness. You won't have any trouble getting them to study—the problem will be to get them to do anything else! They'll be very concerned with "book knowledge" at this point, and with "form."

They may write very detailed, very precise, wonderful rituals, with no concern whatsoever for the "spark" and energy needed to make a ritual effective. They'll probably get over it. Some of them never do. I know High Priests and High Priestesses who are, as we say, still glowing orange.

Your biggest problem here will be the Vice and Virtue, Dishonesty and Truthfulness. When students screw up here, they do it on a grand scale. I had four students who decided around this stage that they had the right to decide whether another student should be advanced. They believed they were perfectly justified in making this decision, and without hesitation, told me they refused to advance him. This is after they had a secret meeting with him, telling him that it was about me, and then challenging him to prove to them that he knew enough to advance.

I don't know how they came to the conclusion that they had a right to do this, but they did. They were surprised at my reaction. When they told other teachers what they'd done, they were amazed at those reactions, too. (As a rule, the reaction was "You did WHAT!?!?")

This is, of course, an extreme example of the Vice of Dishonesty. They were obviously deluding themselves. In a strange way, though, they were honest with me—they did come out and face me.

Netzach is Fire grade, and all hell breaks loose here, for Netzach is the Sphere of Emotion. Talk about "letting it all hang out!" This is a time to keep a tight rein on your students, placing a special emphasis on ethics, logic, etc. Suddenly the spark that was missing in their spells and rituals is there. Everything begins to work better. Remember that Netzach is a reflection of Geburah, and students get a mini-Vision of Power here, without having gone through the balance of Tifareth. You'll know things have calmed down when the Virtue of Unselfishness comes through.

After Fire grade, we give First Degree.

The experienced teachers among you will have realized at this point that all these phases sound familiar. Their students have gone through these stages in their growth, as indeed have the teachers, whether or not they have ever seen the glyph of the Tree of Life or read a book on Qabala!

These phases can be seen in all aspects of life, not just the spiritual. A young High Priest I know was bemoaning the actions of some members of his group who had apparently been amused by the Sphere of Illusion. We discussed these theories and the light bulb coming on over his head was almost visible. "When I was 14," he said, "I hit the Sphere of Illusion and thought I knew everything. Boy, was I wrong!"

Mark Twain said it best:

> When I was a boy of fourteen, my father was so ignorant I could hardly stand to have the old man around. But when I got to be twenty-one, I was astonished at how much he had learned in seven years.[2]

At this point, your students have made a strong effort to work on all planes which deal with the personality, on all four Elements within. This is not to say they will never need to tread these paths again. We all travel them many times, but a student who has reached First Degree has made a tremendous effort toward balance and growth.

---

[2] Mark Twain, *Roughing It* (New York: NAL/Dutton, 1962).

When and if students approach Second Degree—Tifareth—
the Vice of False Pride sets in. Students are changing into teachers and can be disgustingly aware of how much they've learned
and grown. They are, unfortunately, unaware of how much
learning and growing remains to be done.

This is known as the "Pompous Ass Stage." Students at this
level behave in a very superior manner toward less advanced students (and even toward the teacher) and are given to such patronizing statements as "I won't even try to explain it to you
because you are not capable of understanding." This is not only
extremely irritating, but obviously not the proper attitude for a
teacher. When they have calmed down a bit and developed the attitude of sharing, of helping, they are ready to become teachers.

Between Second Degree and Third Degree, both of which
are Tifareth, is one of the "dark nights of the soul" encountered
in spiritual work. Your guidance, comfort, and help are greatly
needed here. Students could be undergoing what is necessary
for them to have one of the Visions of Tifareth, Understanding
the Mysteries of Sacrifice or Vision of the Harmony of Things.
It does seem that you must go through a great deal in order to
achieve these states of understanding.

This difficult time will be different for each student. Re-
mind them that they'll never be given anything they are unable
to bear. Be there for them. It's all you can do.

During all these growing phases, the Qabala can be used
to guide your students. You cannot teach them the Mysteries,
but you can lead them to their own awareness, through the use
of Magical Images, symbols, and correspondences inherent in
the Qabala. Even if you only use the Magical Images, you'll
make great strides and so will they.

A special hint if you use the Tree as a guide: Just as you cannot leave a room completely without entering another, so students often cannot complete the work in one sphere unless they
move to the next. If a student seems stuck in a sphere, move him
or her forward by suggesting meditations on the sphere to come.

Specific problems which occur at any stage, outside the
normal difficulties that come with the energies invoked, can be

helped with the use of the Tree. When a problem becomes apparent, you can suggest work on the sphere which will counteract the difficulty. If a student is too dry, too logical (if that's possible—Mr. Spock wouldn't think so), too wrapped up in book knowledge, work on Netzach could be helpful. Someone ruled by emotion could use work with Hod. Work with Yesod can strengthen the intuition and memory, as can work on the 32nd path. The information in Appendix III (page 181) shows the spheres that will help with other problems.

GROUP MEDITATIONS

While personal meditations are not only encouraged but insisted upon in our tradition, group meditations are an important part of our training program.

Mantras

The Mantra Meditation is effective as a group exercise and as a solitary one, and fits easily into a ritual. If you have a small group, you can prepare a tape with the mantra repeated rhythmically for about ten minutes. Played as a background, it will help the students keep the chant and rhythm going as you instruct them on any visualization you wish to use.

If you have a large group, two volunteers can chant the mantra softly. With two, the chant remains constant when the chanters need to breathe.

Pathworkings

Guided meditations are journeys on the paths between the spheres. Dolores Ashcroft-Nowicki has some excellent ones in her book, *The Shining Paths.*[3] There are four in my book, *The Witches Tarot.*[4]

---

[3] Dolores Ashcroft-Nowicki, *The Shining Paths: An Experience in Vision of the 12 Paths of the Tree of Life* (Wellingborough, England: Aquarian Press, 1983).
[4] Ellen Cannon Reed, *The Witches Tarot* (St. Paul, MN: Llewellyn, 1989).

It is possible to create your own. Using the correspondences found in Appendix I (page 145), create a journey that begins in one of the spheres, using the appropriate tarot card as a door to the path, and traveling toward the next sphere.

Temples

One way to expose your students to the energies of the spheres is to conduct your classes in the temple of the appropriate sphere. Four such temples are described in Appendix II (page 173). Describe the temple slowly to the class, letting them share in the visualization.

Conduct your class as usual, pausing once or twice to go over the visualization again. As your students' skills in visualization develop, there will be no need to repeat the description. When the class is over, all of you should see the temple fading away to be replaced by the "real" location.

Rituals

As we are all aware, different rituals have different meanings and therefore use different forms of energy. A High Priestess or High Priest directs and controls the energies brought into the rite. The Qabala provides a very simple way of bringing into the circle the precise energy of the exact aspect of the Lord and/or Lady you wish to use.

Suppose you are performing a Moon rite, New or Full. You have a group that is not too advanced, and you do not wish to draw the full force of the Goddess at her most impersonal unknowable aspect. You want the gentle, loving power of the Moon.

After you've created your circle, picture the Tree before you (you can use a picture if you like) and imagine an influx of power from the Ain Soph to Kether. The energy flows down the Tree, sphere by sphere, until it reaches Yesod. At this point, see the violet energy filling your circle with Moon power. You are now ready to continue your rite, in a circle filled with the energy of the Sphere of the Moon.

A more advanced group, whose visualization skills have developed, can handle a slightly different method. Let them share the visualization with you, but this time, fill the circles with the colors of Malkuth, starting with the planetary colors and working up through the Four Worlds. When you have reached the deity color, let the whole group see the circle moving toward Yesod, entering it. Conduct the rest of your circle in the Sphere of the Moon. You will feel a definite difference in the two rituals.

If you have a specific purpose other than worship, one which requires other than Moon energy, start as I have described, but fill the circle with the color of the proper sphere in the first method, or move your circle to the sphere in the second. A healing rite would use energy drawn from Tifareth, for example. The circle would be filled with a Sun-yellow light.

In Appendix VI (page 189), you'll find a rite using both Qabalistic and Craft symbolism. The energies of four spheres and the energies of the elements are invoked, in order to cure dissension between two members of a circle. A study of this rite shows how easily the two can be intertwined.

USING THE QABALA AS A TRAINING STRUCTURE

If you wish to use the Qabala, as the Western Isian tradition does, as a framework for your coven's training program, I encourage you to do so. I've spoken briefly of the way we use it. Below, I've listed the subjects my coven teaches in the appropriate spheres and the requirements it has for each grade. You will make your own decisions as to what arrangements are appropriate, but this will give you a starting place.

Neophyte

Basic knowledge about the workings of the coven, its elemental correspondences, meditation techniques, circle casting, Wheel of the Year, developing personal relationships with the gods.

Earth (Malkuth)

Basic magical techniques, stones and crystals, herbs, basic astrology, basic information on the gods of Egypt. Some sort of Earth project is necessary, usually the making of an oil or incense for the use of the coven. Students must also write a paper on a deity with whom they have worked to develop a personal relationship.

Air (Yesod)

Qabala. Tarot as a meditational tool. This usually takes up the whole time. Another god/dess paper is required.

Water (Hod)

The tarot as a divination tool. Other forms of divination. Students are required to become competent with two divination forms, one of which must be tarot and one of which must be new. The components of ritual and how to put one together. Another god/dess paper is required although the student may submit a ritual instead.

Fire (Netzach)

Leading rituals. Aspecting (serving as a vessel for the Lord or Lady). Students are required to aspect both a god and a goddess of their choice, and also to invoke a god and a goddess into another student. The duties and obligations of a priest/ess. Students should, at this time, choose a deity to whom they wish to make a special dedication when they take their First Degree, and to choose their Inner Circle Name. Another god/dess paper. The final requirement is to lead a Moon rite.

First Degree (Netzach)

With this, the student becomes an initiate, a priest/ess, a brother or sister of the Wicca. Students are expected to continue the magical studies begun in the earlier grades. During the first twelve months after First Degree, a priest/ess shall also complete a priesthood project as a contribution to the coven. This can take many forms. A First Degree witch will take a more active part in the performance of rituals, will lead some of them, and may be asked to assist in the training of new students.

We don't require students to go further, nor is such advancement to further degrees automatic.

Second Degree (Tifareth)

Second Degree is a total dedication of one's self to the Goddess and the God.

Third Degree (Tifareth)

With this initiation, the witch becomes an Elder of the Western Isian tradition. A Third may hive off and form a new coven, although it is not a requirement.

What I have listed here is really not all the work that is done. Special work, exercises, and meditations will be required, as will personal work on specific problems in development.

The ceremonies signifying entrance into each elemental grade are very important, signaling as they do the beginning of work in a new element and a new sphere. You will want to develop special ceremonies for these occasions. Ours were originally cut down versions of Golden Dawn rituals, but over the years, they've changed so much that I doubt the Golden Dawn would recognize them.

The more you study and use the Qabala, the more ideas you will find. As you grow, the Tree grows. There is an unending source of knowledge, guidance, strength, and joy in the Tree of Life, and it is available to you, if only you wish to have it.

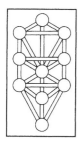

19

THE END AND
THE BEGINNING

*All things began in order, so shall they end, and so shall
begin again.*

—Sir Thomas Browne[1]

THE SYMBOLISM OF THE Qabala is all around us, if we
will look and see. Unintentionally, the world arranges itself
qabalistically.

A traffic light goes from green (Netzach, Pillar of Force),
to yellow (Tifareth, the Mediator, on the Middle Pillar), to red
(Geburah, Pillar of Restriction).

Trees are green in their expansive cycle, and change to reds
and oranges in their Geburah cycles.

I have friends who feel that the most common arrangement of the elements in a circle (see below) reflects "ceremonial

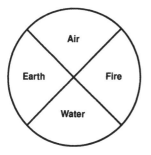

---

[1] Sir Thomas Browne, "The Garden of Cyrus," chapter 5, *The Oxford Dictionary of Quotations* (London: Oxford University Press, 1983), p. 95.

magic" attributions. They prefer the second order shown. I do, of course, respect their beliefs and giggles, but I must give a teeny giggle, because their order of elements fits in exactly with the three pillars and Malkuth shown here.

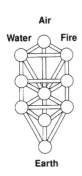

Air
Water **Fire**
Earth

At a science fiction convention, I participated in a panel on "Real Magic." Another panelist, author Jon deCles, pointed out that *The Dark Crystal* was a Qabalistic movie. The ten evil (but strong) skeksis represented the Pillar of Severity. The ten gentle (but ineffectual) mystics were the Pillar of Mercy.

Unbalanced Mercy is weakness . . . unbalanced Severity is cruelty.

The crystal itself was unholy because it was not complete, just as the Tree of Life would be incomplete if it lacked any one of its spheres. When the skeksis and mystics were rejoined in the movie and the missing shard replaced in the crystal, balance (the Middle Pillar) was achieved and all was well.

Throughout life, through all phases of life, we go through the stages outlined in the Qabala, whether we study Qabala or not. The specific information dealing with energies, theology, and thealogy, and all aspects of the world beyond physical manifestation can be understood more clearly with the use of the Tree.

Using the symbolic arrangement represented by the Tree is not a matter of forcing symbolism on you, but a recognition and understanding of a pattern that already exists.

Joining this information to the joy and love found in the Craft of the Wise Ones, or any of the pagan philosophies, gives us a beautiful and effective way of guiding spiritual growth. I, for one, would find Qabala and other ceremonial magic techniques much too somber without the added aspects of paganism. Without Qabala, I would not have the direction I have as a student, teacher, and seeker.

In the following Appendices, I've organized the material discussed in previous chapters, and added further information. I encourage you to try this information, use it, give it a chance to enter your mind and heart. Let me share them with you.

Blessed be!

> The Kingdom
> Finds its Foundation
> In Splendor and Victory.
> Beauty is the balance
> Of Might and Mercy.
> Understanding and Wisdom
> Will lead me to the Crown.

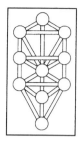

APPENDIX I:
THE SPHERES, THE PATHS, AND THEIR CORRESPONDENCES

FOR THE SPHERES, the information on the following pages includes: Hebrew and English names, a quote from the *Sepher Yetzirah* (The Book of Formation) as translated by W. Wynn Westcott,[1] the Magical Image, the Name of Power, the Archangel, the Angels (Hebrew and English names,) Planetary Attribution, the Virtue, the Vice, Titles, Spiritual Experience, the Flashing Colors (the colors of the Four Worlds), Symbols, Deities (examples of the deities who can be placed here, but certainly not an exhaustive list), Precious Stones, Plants, Perfumes, and Animals.

For the paths, the following pages include: the Tarot card, the Flashing Colors, the Astrological Attribution, the Animal, and the Jewel.

MALKUTH — THE KINGDOM

"The Tenth Path is called the Resplendent Intelligence, because it is exalted above every head, and sits upon the Throne of *Binah*. . . . It illuminates the splendours of all the lights, and causes a supply of influence to emanate from the Prince of countenances," the Angel of Kether.

Magical Image: A young woman, crowned and throned.

---

[1] W. Wynn Westcott, *Sepher Yetzirah* (New York: Samuel Weiser, 1975), pp. 28–29.

Name of Power: Adonai (Adonath) ha Aretz (Lord/Lady of Earth), Adonai Malekh (Lord King).

Archangel: Sandolphon.

Angels: Kerubim, the Strong.

Planetary Attribution: Earth, the planet.

Virtue: Discrimination.

Vice: Inertia.

Titles: The Gate, Kallah, The Bride, The Gate of Death, The Inferior Mother, The Gate of Justice, Malkah, The Queen, The Gate of Tears.

Spiritual Experience: Vision of the Holy Guardian Angel.

Deity Color: Yellow.

Archangel Colors: Ochre, Russet, Olive, Black.

Angel Colors: Ochre, Russet, Olive, Black flecked with gold.

Planetary Color: Black, rayed with yellow.

Symbols: Altar of the Double Cube, The Triangle of Art, The equal-armed cross, The magic circle.

Deities: Earth and grain deities: Pan, Ceres, Demeter, Geb, Marduk, Nisaba, Nrthus, Mati-Syra-Zemba, Yorillo, Pellevvinen, Prithvi, Tekketskerkok, Nokomis, Ethinoha, Onathe, Chicomecoatl, Niamh, Cernunnos, Myrddin.

Precious Stone: Rock crystal.

Plants: Willow, lily, ivy.

Perfume: Dittany of Crete.

Illusion: Materialism.

Obligation: Discipline.

Briatic Correspondence: Stability.

YESOD – THE FOUNDATION

"The Ninth Path is called the Pure Intelligence, so called because it purifies the Numerations, it proves and corrects the designing of their representation, and disposes the unity with which they are combined without diminution or division."

Magical Image: A beautiful naked man, very strong.

Name of Power: Shaddai El Chai, Almighty Living One.

Archangel: Gabriel.

Angels: Aishim, the Souls of Fire.

Planetary Attribution: The Moon.

Virtue: Independence.

Vice: Idleness.

Titles: Treasurehouse of Images, the Sphere of Illusion.

Spiritual Experience: Vision of the Machinery of the Universe.

Deity Color: Indigo.

Archangel Color: Violet.

Angel Color: Very dark purple.

Planetary Color: Citrine, flecked with azure.

Symbols: The perfumes and the sandals, the mirror.

Deities: All Moon deities: Goda, Diana, Thoth, Ganesha, Hecate, Sin, Myestats, Kuu, Mah, Varuna, Soma, Ch'ango, Hengo, Tsuki-yomie, Pah, Coyolxauhqui, Quilla, Auchimalgen.

Precious Stone: Quartz.

Plants: Mandrake, banyan, damiana.

Perfumes: Jasmine, ginseng, all fragrant roots.

Animals: Elephant, tortoise, toad.

Illusion: Security.

Obligation: Trust.

Briatic Correspondences: Receptivity, perception.

HOD—SPLENDOR, GLORY

"The Eighth Path is called the Absolute or Perfect, because it is the means of the primordial, which has no root by which it can cleave nor rest, except in the hidden places of *Gedulah, Magnificence*, which emanate from its own proper essence."

Magical Image: A hermaphrodite.

Name of Power: Elohim Tzabaoth (God/dess of Hosts).

Archangels: Michael, Raphael.

Angels: Beni Elohim (God/dess of Hosts).

Planetary Attribution: Mercury.

Virtue: Truthfulness.

Vice: Falsehood, dishonesty.

Titles: The Lesser Temple.

Spiritual Experience: Vision of Splendor.

Deity Color: Violet, purple.

Archangel Color: Orange.

Angel Color: Russet red.

Planetary Color: Yellowish-black, flecked with white.

Symbols: Names, mantras, caduceus.

Deities: Messengers and teachers: Tehuti (Thoth), Hermes, Mercury, Tautes, Anubis, Ogma.

Precious Stone: Opal.

Plant: Moly.

Perfume: Storax (liquidambar gum).

Animals: Jackal, twin serpents.

Illusion: Order.

Obligation: Learning.

Briatic Correspondence: Abstraction.

NETZACH—VICTORY

"The Seventh Path is called the Occult Intelligence, because it is the Refulgent Splendour of the Intellectual virtues which are perceived by the eyes of the intellect, and by the contemplation of faith."

Magical Image: A beautiful naked woman.

Name of Power: Yahveh Tzabaoth (Lord of Hosts).

Archangel: Haniel.

Angels: Elohim.

Planetary Attribution: Venus.

Virtue: Unselfishness.

Vices: Unchastity, lust for power.

Spiritual Experiences: Firmness, valor.

Deity Color: Amber.

Archangel Color: Emerald.

Angel Color: Bright yellowish-green.

Planetary Color: Olive, flecked with gold.

Symbols: Lamp, girdle, the rose.

Deities: All love deities: Venus, Ishtar, Aphrodite, Hathor, Rhiannon, Niamh, Olwen, Cerridwen (for inspiration).

Precious Stone: Emerald.

Plant: Rose.

Perfumes: Rose, benzoin, red sandalwood.

Animal: Lynx.

Illusion: Projection.

Obligation: Responsibility.

Briatic Correspondence: Nurture.

TIFARETH—BEAUTY, HARMONY

"The Sixth Path is called the Intelligence of the Mediating Influence, because in it are multiplied the influxes of the emanations, for it causes that influence to flow into all reservoirs of the Blessings, with which they themselves are united."

Magical Image: A king, a child, a sacrificed god.

Name of Power: Yahveh Eloah Va Daath (God/dess made manifest in the Sphere of the Mind.

Archangels: Raphael, Michael.

Angels: Malachim, the kings.

Planetary Attribution: The Sun.

Virtue: Devotion to the Great Work.

Vice: False pride.

Titles: The Lesser Countenance.

Spiritual Experience: Vision of the harmony of things, understanding the mysteries of sacrifice.

Deity Color: Clear rose-pink.

Archangel Color: Yellow.

Angel Color: Rich salmon-pink.

Planetary Color: Golden amber.

Symbols: The red cross, the Calvary cross, the truncated pyramid, the lamen, the cube.

Deities: Sun deities, holy children, healers, sacrificed kings, illuminators: Osiris, Apollo, Attis, Adonis, Tammuz, Balder, Bran, Llew, Lugh, Gwern, Jesus, Dionysius, Balin, Ogma, Bride, Nonens, Shamas, Mot, Dozhbog, Parva, Huare-Khasaeta, Sura, Amaterasu, Koodjanuk, Shakuru, Tezcatlipoca, Inti, Apu, Panchai, Ra, Sekhmet.

Precious Stones: Topaz, yellow diamond.

Plants: Acacia, bay laurel, vine.

Perfume: Olibanum (frankincense).

Animals: Phoenix, lion, pelican in piety.

Illusion: Identification.

Obligation: Integrity.

Briatic Correspondences: Centrality, wholeness.

GEBURAH—MIGHT

"The Fifth Path is called the Radical Intelligence, because it is itself the essence equal to the Unity, uniting itself to the Binah, or Intelligence which emanates from the Primordial depths of Wisdom or Chokmah, Wisdom."

Magical Image: A mighty warrior in a chariot.

Name of Power: Elohim Gibor, Mighty God/dess.

Archangel: Khamael.

Angels: Seraphim, Fiery Serpents.

Planetary Attribution: Mars.

Virtues: Energy, courage.

Vices: Cruelty, wanton destruction.

Titles: Pachad, Fear, Din, Justice.

Spiritual Experience: Vision of Power.

Deity Color: Orange.

Archangel Color: Scarlet.

Angel Color: Bright scarlet.

Planetary Color: Red, flecked with black.

Symbols: The pentagon, the sword, the spear, the scourge, the chain, the five-petalled Tudor rose.

Deities: War, protector, and avenger deities, smith and forge deities: Mars, Ares, Bran, Brigid, Minerva/Athena, Kali, the Morrigan, Lugh, Tubal Cain, Vulcan, Hephaestes, Ningurs, Culan, Odin, Vali, Pyerun, Indra, Lei Kung, Okun-Nush, Huitzilopochtl.

Precious Stone: Ruby.

Plants: Oak, nettle.

Perfume: Tobacco.

Animal: Basilisk.

Illusion: Invincibility.

Obligations: Courage and loyalty.

Briatic Correspondence: Power.

CHESED—MERCY

"The Fourth Path is named Measuring, Cohesive or Receptacular; and is so called because it contains all the holy powers, and from it emanate all the spiritual virtues with the most exalted essences: they emanate one from the other by the power of the primordial emanation. [The Highest Crown]." Kether.

Magical Image: A mighty crowned and throned king.

Name of Power: El (God).

Archangel: Tzadkiel.

Angels: Chasmalim, the Brilliant Ones.

Planetary Attribution: Jupiter.

Virtue: Obedience.

Vices: Bigotry, hypocrisy, gluttony.

Titles: Gedulah, Love, Majesty, Magnificence.

Spiritual Experience: Vision of Love.

Deity Color: Deep violet.

Archangel Color: Blue.

Angel Color: Deep purple.

Planetary Color: Deep azure-flecked yellow.

Symbols: The solid figure, orb, wand, the tetradron, sceptre, crook.

Deities: Benevolent ruler gods: Jupiter, Odin as lawgiver, Nodens, etc.

Precious Stones: Amethyst, sapphire, lapis lazuli.

Plants: Olive, shamrock.

Perfume: Cedar.

Animal: Unicorn.

Illusion: Self-righteousness.

Obligation: Humility.

Briatic Correspondence: Authority.

BINAH—UNDERSTANDING

"The Third Path is the Sanctifying Intelligence, and is the basis of foundation of Primordial Wisdom, which is called the Former of Faith, and its roots, Amen; and it is the parent of Faith from whose virtues doth Faith emanate."

Magical Image: A mature woman.

Name of Power: Yahveh Elohim.

Archangel: Tzafkiel.

Angels: Aralim, the Thrones.

Planetary Attribution: Saturn.

Virtue: Silence.

Vice: Avarice.

Titles: Ama, the dark sterile mother; Aima, the bright fertile mother; Marah, the great sea; Khorsia, the throne.

Spiritual Experience: Vision of Sorrow.

Deity Color: Crimson.

Archangel Color: Black.

Angel Color: Dark brown.

Planetary Color: Gray flecked with pink.

Symbols: The Yoni, the cup or chalice.

Deities: Mother goddesses, crones, Saturnian deities: Goda, Goida, Tautus (Tautatis) Olwen, Danu, Isis, Demeter, Tiamat, Kishar, Asherat, Gefjon, Parvati, Atira, Akna, Bran, Chronos, Nut.

Precious Stones: Star sapphire, pearl.

Plants: Cypress, lotus, lily.

Perfume: Myrrh.

Animal: Bee.

Illusion: Death.

Briatic Correspondence: Comprehension.

CHOKMAH—WISDOM

"The Second Path is that of the Illuminating Intelligence; it is the Crown of Creation, the Splendour of the Unity, equalling it, and it is exalted above every head, and named by the Kabalists the Second Glory."

Magical Image: A bearded male figure.

Name of Power: Yahveh or Yah, Lord.

Archangel: Ratzkiel.

Angels: Auphanim, the Wheels.

Planetary Attribution: The zodiac.

Virtue: Devotion.

Vice: —

Titles: Power of Yetzirah, Ab, Abba, the Supernal Father.

Spiritual Experience: Vision of the Source We Seek.

Deity Color: Pure soft blue.

Archangel Color: Gray.

Angel Color: Pearl gray, iridescent.

Planetary Color: White-flecked yellow.

Symbols: The phallus, yod, the tower, the straight line.

Deities: All Father gods, god/desses of wisdom, Priapic Gods: Zeus, Jupiter, Great Pan, Osiris, the Dagda, Cernnunos, Tubal Can, Nuada (Nodens), Enki, Ashur, Ivarog, Izanagi, Tirawa, Udakanda, Geb.

Precious Stones: Star ruby, turquoise.

Plant: Amaranth.

Perfume: Musk.

Animal: Man.

Illusion: Independence.

Briatic Correspondence: Revolution.

KETHER—THE CROWN

"The First Path is called the Admirable or the Hidden Intelligence (the Highest Crown) for it is the Light giving the power of comprehension of the First Principle which has no beginning; and it is the Primal Glory, for no created being can attain to its essence."

Magical Image: An ancient bearded king seen in profile.

Name of Power: Ehieih, I am.

Archangel: Metatron.

Angels: Chioth ha Qadesh, Holy Living Creatures.

Planetary Attribution: First swirlings.

Virtue: Attainment, completion of the Great Work.

Vice: —

Titles: Existence of Existences, Ancient of Days, the White Head, Macroprosopos, the Vast Countenance, Lux Occulta (the Hidden Light).

Spiritual Experience: Reunion with the Source.

Deity Color: Brilliance.

Archangel Color: Pure white brilliance.

Angel Color: Pure white brilliance.

Planetary Color: White-flecked gold.

Symbols: The point, the swastika, the crown, point within a circle.

Deities: All creator/creatrix deities: Ptah, Gaea, Jumala, Nipara, Nohochacyum, Ngai, Cagn.

Precious Stone: Diamond.

Plant: Flowering almond.

Perfume: Ambergris.

Animals: The swan, the hawk.

Illusion: Attainment.

Briatic Correspondence: Unity.

THE PATHS

11th Path—Between Kether and Chokmah

Card: The Fool.

Letter: Aleph.

Deity Color: Bright pale yellow.

Archangel Color: Sky blue.

Angel Color: Blue-emerald.

Planetary Color: Emerald-flecked gold.

Astrological Attribution: Air.

Animal: Eagle.

Jewel: Chalcedony.

12th Path—Between Kether and Binah

Card: The Magician.

Letter: Beth.

Deity Color: Yellow.

Archangel Color: Purple.

Angel Color: Gray.

Planetary Color: Violet-flecked indigo.

Astrological Attribution: Mercury.

Animal: Ibis.

Jewel: Agate.

13th Path—Between Kether and Tifareth

Card: The High Priestess.

Letter: Gimel.

Deity Color: Blue.

Archangel Color: Silver.

Angel Color: Cold pale blue.

Planetary Color: Silver rayed with blue.

Astrological Attribution: The Moon.

Animal: Camel.

Jewel: Moonstone, pearl.

14th Path—Between Chokmah and Binah

Card: The Empress.

Letter: Daleth.

Deity Color: Emerald green.

Archangel Color: Sky blue.

Angel Color: Early spring green.

Planetary Color: Bright rose or cerise rayed with pale green.

Astrological Attribution: Venus.

Animal: Sparrow, dove.

Jewel: Emerald.

15th Path—Between Chokmah and Tifareth

Card: The Emperor.

Letter: Heh.

Deity Color: Scarlet.

Archangel Color: Red.

Angel Color: Brilliant flame.

Planetary Color: Glowing red.

Astrological Attribution: Aries.

Animal: Ram.

Jewel: Ruby.

16th Path—Between Chokmah and Chesed

Card: The High Priest.

Letter: Vau.

Deity Color: Red-orange.

Archangel Color: Deep indigo.

Angel Color: Deep warm olive.

Planetary Color: Rich brown.

Astrological Attribution: Taurus.

Animal: Bull.

Jewel: Topaz.

17th Path—Between Binah and Tifareth

Card: The Lovers.

Letter: Zain.

Deity Color: Orange.

Archangel Color: Pale mauve.

Angel Color: New yellow leather.

Planetary Color: Reddish gray, inclined to mauve.

Astrological Attribution: Gemini.

Animal: Magpie.

Jewel: Alexandrite.

18th Path—Between Binah and Geburah

Card: The Chariot.

Letter: Cheth.

Deity Color: Amber.

Archangel Color: Maroon.

Angel Color: Rich bright russet.

Planetary Color: Dark greenish-brown.

Astrological Attribution: Cancer.

Animal: Sphinx.

Jewel: Amber.

19th Path—Between Geburah and Chesed

Card: Strength.

Letter: Teth.

Deity Color: Greenish-yellow.

Archangel Color: Deep purple.

Angel Color: Gray.

Planetary Color: Reddish-yellow.

Astrological Attribution: Leo.

Animal: Lioness.

Jewel: Cat's eye, citrine.

20th Path—Between Chesed and Tifareth

Card: The Seeker (the Hermit).

Letter: Yod.

Deity Color: Yellowish-green.

Archangel Color: Slate gray.

Angel Color: Green-gray.

Planetary Color: Plum.

Astrological Attribution: Virgo.

Animal: Virgin, hermit.

Jewel: Peridot.

21st Path—Between Chesed and Netzach

Card: The Wheel of Fortune.

Letter: Kaph.

Deity Color: Violet.

Archangel Color: Blue.

Angel Color: Rich purple.

Planetary Color: Bright blue rayed with yellow.

Astrological Attribution: Jupiter.

Animal: Eagle.

Jewel: Lapis lazuli, amethyst.

22nd Path—Between Geburah and Tifareth

Card: Justice.

Letter: Lamed.

Deity Color: Emerald blue.

Archangel Color: Blue.

Angel Color: Deep blue-green.

Planetary Color: Pale green.

Astrological Attribution: Libra.

Animal: Spider.

Jewel: Bloodstone.

23rd Path — Between Geburah and Hod

Card: The Hanged Man.

Letter: Mem.

Deity Color: Deep blue.

Archangel Color: Sea-green.

Angel Color: Deep olive-green.

Planetary Color: White-flecked purple.

Astrological Attribution: Water.

Animal: Eagle, snake, scorpion.

Jewel: Aquamarine.

24th Path — Between Tifareth and Netzach

Card: Death.

Letter: Nun.

Deity Color: Green-blue.

Archangel Color: Dull brown.

Angel Color: Very dark brown.

Planetary Color: Vivid indigo-brown.

Astrological Attribution: Scorpio.

Animal: Scarab.

Jewel: Carved scarab.

NEZACH HOD

25th Path—Between ~~Tifareth~~ and ~~Yesod~~

Card: The Tower.

Letter: Samech.

Deity Color: Blue.

Archangel Color: Yellow.

Angel Color: Green.

Planetary Color: Dark vivid blue.

Astrological Attribution: Sagittarius.

Animal: Centaur, horse.

Jewel: Obsidian.

26th Path—Between Tifareth and Hod

Card: The Horned One.

Letter: Ayin.

Deity Color: Indigo.

Archangel Color: Black.

Angel Color: Blue-black.

Planetary Color: Cold, very dark gray.

Astrological Attribution: Capricorn.

Animal: Goat.

Jewel: Black diamond.

TIPHGATH   YCSOD

27th Path—Between ~~Netzach~~ and ~~Hod~~

Card: Temperance.

Letter: Peh.

Deity Color: Scarlet.

Archangel Color: Red.

Angel Color: Venetian red.

Planetary Color: Bright red, rayed with azure and emerald.

Astrological Attribution: Mars.

Animal: Horse, bear, wolf.

Jewel: Any red stone.

28th Path—Between Netzach and Yesod

Card: The Stars.

Letter: Tzaddi.

Deity Color: Violet.

Archangel Color: Blue.

Angel Color: Bluish mauve.

Planetary Color: White-tinged purple.

Astrological Attribution: Aquarius.

Animal: Man, eagle.

Jewel: Chalcedony.

29th Path—Between Netzach and Malkuth

Card: The Moon.

Letter: Qoph.

Deity Color: Crimson.

Archangel Color: Buff flecked with silver-white.

Angel Color: Light translucent pinkish-brown.

Planetary Color: Stone.

Astrological Attribution: Pisces.

Animal: Fish, dolphin.

Jewel: Pearl.

30th Path—Between Hod and Yesod

Card: The Sun.

Letter: Resh.

Deity Color: Orange.

Archangel Color: Gold-yellow.

Angel Color: Rich amber.

Planetary Color: Amber, rayed with red.

Astrological Attribution: The Sun.

Animal: Lion, sparrowhawk.

Jewel: Chrysoleth.

31st Path—Between Hod and Malkuth

Card: Judgement.

Letter: Shin.

Deity Color: Glowing orange-scarlet.

Archangel Color: Vermillion.

Angel Color: Scarlet, flecked with gold.

Planetary Color: Vermillion, flecked with crimson and emerald.

Astrological Attribution: Fire.

Animal: Lion.

Jewel: Fire opal.

32nd Path — Between Yesod and Malkuth

Card: The Universe.

Letter: Tav.

Deity Color: Indigo.

Archangel Color: Black.

Angel Color: Blue-black.

Planetary Color: Black, rayed with blue.

Astrological Attribution: Saturn.

Animal: Crocodile.

Jewel: Smoky quartz.

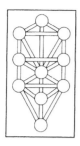

APPENDIX II: THE ASTRAL TEMPLES

THESE DESCRIPTIONS OF the temples of the four lowest spheres have many uses. You can use them to learn more about the sphere they represent, or use them as starting places for pathworkings. Feel free to add or change anything that will make the temple more personal for you, or more effective. Visualizing yourself in one of these temples, and then meditating on a symbol or image connected with that sphere can bring excellent results.

THE TEMPLE OF MALKUTH

The floor is made up of black and white squares. In the center of the temple is a black altar, a double cube (one on top of the other) draped with a white cloth (see figure A.1, page 174). On this altar you will find four candles in the colors of the elements, and symbols of each element, each in its proper quadrant.

You can see pillars around the circumference of the temple, but you cannot see beyond them to the walls. To the east, you see two large pillars, a black one on the left and a white one on the right. Beyond and between those pillars, you see a representation of the Universe Card of the tarot, as large as a door. Above the card is a silvery symbol of the Moon.

To the left of the black pillar, and beyond it, you see an equally large representation of the Judgment card and above it, a symbol of Mercury.

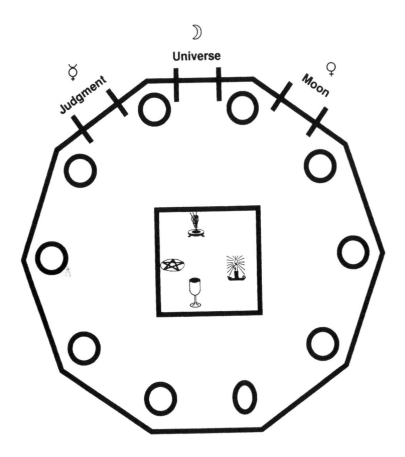

Figure A.1.   Temple of Malkuth.

To the right of and beyond the white pillar, you see a door-sized representation of the Moon card, surmounted by a symbol of Venus. Between the other pillars are statues of various gods and goddesses with small altars before them. If you wish to commune with one of them, you have only to go to the altar and meditate.

If you wish to meditate on the Magical Image, formulate it between the black and white pillars.

THE TEMPLE OF YESOD

The temple has nine sides and is made of quartz (see figure A.2, page 176). In its center is a crescent-shaped altar, draped in violet. Behind the altar is a pedestal on which you may visualize the Magical Image if you desire to meditate on it.

The floor of the temple is ever-changing shades of violet, lavender, and purple. The temple has no roof, and receives its light from the Moon. Around the walls are altars to various Moon deities. You may approach any that you wish to contact.

The temple has four doors, arranged as in the figure A.2 (page 176). Each is represented by a tarot card, and above each door is a planetary symbol. The statues and altar trappings seem very elusive—their shapes and postures change as you watch.

More than the temple of any other sphere, this temple is affected by your thoughts. If you do not see a statue representing the god or goddess you wish to adore, simply turn to an altar and picture that deity above it.

The doors out of the temple waver. Should you desire to exit through one of them, use the power of your mind to make the door firmly visible.

THE TEMPLE OF HOD

This temple has eight sides. There are five doors, each with a different tarot card, and each with a different planetary symbol above it (see figure A.3, page 177). The altar is opal with orange draperies. There is the fragrance of storax in the air.

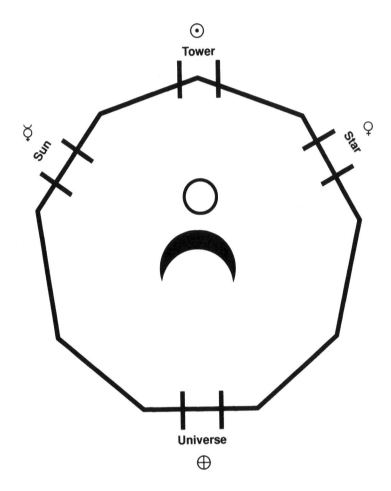

Figure A.2.   Temple of Yesod.

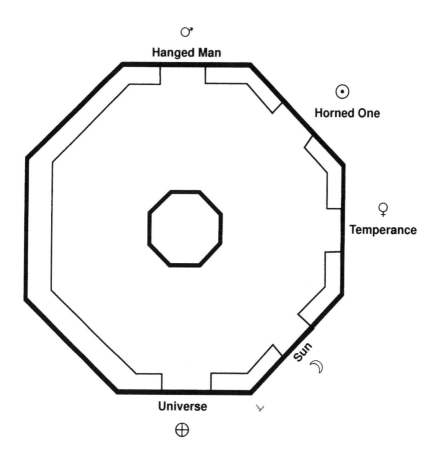

Figure A.3.   Temple of Hod.

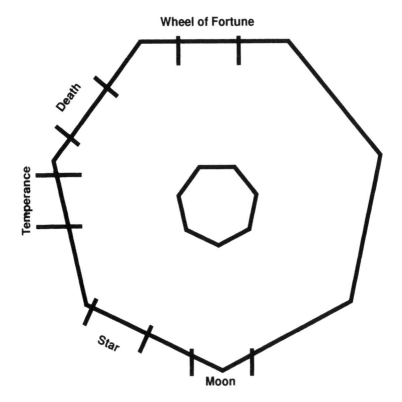

Figure A.4.   Netzach.

Between the doors, filling shelves on every wall, are writings of every sort: books, scrolls, stone tablets, some incredibly ancient, some obviously new.

In front of the eight-sided opal altar is a pedestal. There you may form the Magical Image or representation of the deity you wish to adore.

THE TEMPLE OF NETZACH

The temple has seven sides, although it has only narrow supports (see figure A.4, page 178). It is surrounded by growing things, the green leaves making up the walls of this temple. The seven-sided altar is a large emerald, clear and green. If you gaze into its depths, you will see there either the Magical Image of Netzach, or an image of the deity you wish to adore. Each of the five doors (in this case, openings in the greenery) is a tarot card, with a planetary symbol above it.

The atmosphere here is the quiet of a forest glade, with the quiet broken only by small animal sounds and breezes rustling leaves. Yet you have the feeling of great energy here, hidden life flowing in the breeze, which carries with it the fragrance of roses.

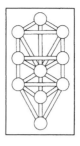

III

APPENDIX III:
THE SPHERES IN
MAGICAL WORK

WHETHER YOU USE THE Qabalistic form of spell casting or any other method, you can use the Planetary Attributions of the spheres to define the sphere you wish to work with.

Work is almost never done with the energies of Kether and Chokmah, and Malkuth is the Sphere of Manifestation, so this Appendix includes only the seven other spheres.

Binah: Comfort in times of sorrow, help with groups, contact with the Goddess unveiled, development of the ability to listen and absorb.

Chesed: Expansion, growth, help from the Ancient Ones, development of punctuality and neatness, anything which deals with order, correction of stinginess, development of stability.

Geburah: Energy, courage, defense, getting rid of the unnecessary, vitality, development of will power and self-discipline.

Tifareth: Honor, power, glory, life, growth, money, healing, illumination.

Netzach: Love in all forms, pleasure, arts, music, creative energy, inspiration, help in overcoming lack of spontaneity, lack of emotion and lack of subjectivity, breaking writer's block and similar problems.

Hod: Business, books, legal judgments, travel information, the intellect, logic, writer's block (the ability to express your thoughts rather than inspiration), curbing over-emotionalism, focus, developing learning or teaching skills, finding teachers and sources of information.

Yesod: Divination, change, understanding flux and reflux, fertility spells, development of intuition, better contact with the unconscious, development of better memory.

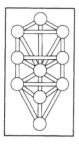

APPENDIX IV: PRONUNCIATION GUIDE

THE HEBREW FOUND in this book and others is transliterated from the Hebrew to the roman alphabet. Most letters can be easily compared, with two exceptions, the Hebrew *cheth* and *tav*.

Cheth in this volume is represented by the letters *ch*, and is pronounced almost as a clearing of the throat, a gutteral sound as found in the Scottish pronunciation of the word *loch*. If you are not sure of the sound, ask a Jewish friend to pronounce "chutzpah."

Tav, in this book, is represented by the letters *th*, but they do not represent the *th*- sound found in such English words as "the" or "thin." *Tav* represents a very breathy *t*, or *t* followed by an *h* sound. "Kether," for example, is pronounced "Ket-her."

    e—as in bet;
    a—as in father;
    i—as in bit;
    o—as in boat;
    u—as in boot.

In the word "Tzabaoth," the *a* after the *b* represents a glottal stop rather than a sound. A glottal stop is the tightening of the throat that makes the difference between "a nice man" and "an ice man." The word could also be written "Tzab'oth," which might be clearer.

As for knowing which syllable to accent, most Hebrew words are accented on the last or next to last syllable. The following words are examples:

KE-ter;
Chok-MAH;
Bin-AH;
Gebur-AH (the *b* in Hebrew is very soft, almost a *v*);
Ti-FAR-eth;
Net-ZACH;
Ye-SOD;
Mal-KUTH;
Elo-HIM;
Da'ATH.

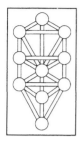

V

APPENDIX V: THE SHARED CROSS

THIS IS A FORM of the Qabalistic cross that is, as the name implies, shared by more than one person(see figure A.5, page 186). It can be used any time sharing is appropriate, such as a handfasting. In its most basic form, it is performed as follows:

Two people join both hands, and one of them speaks as they visualize a ball of light above and between them.

May we share always the light of the Goddess,

The light is seen to come down between them, touching both to their feet.

The Wisdom to be gained in Her Kingdom,

The light is seen crossing between and touching both parties, from the speaker's right shoulder to the left.

Her strength, Her mercy, and Her love.

At the words, "Her love," a sphere of light is seen at the center of the cross and, as the following words are spoken, the sphere grows until it encompasses both persons.

Which is manifest in our love for each other.

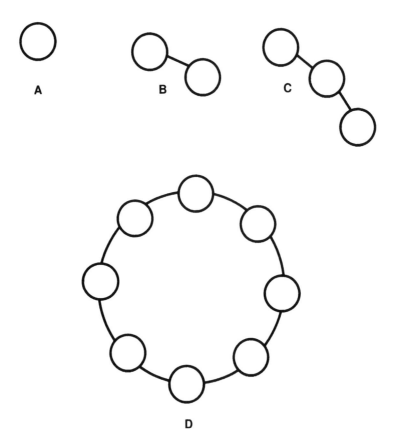

Figure A.5.   Circle-Shared Cross.

THE ALTERNATE SHARED CROSS

This is performed in the same way, except the persons alternate in speaking the words.

A: **May we share always the light of the Goddess:**

B: **The wisdom to be gained in Her Kingdom,**

A: **Her strength,**

B: **Her mercy,**

A: **And Her love,**

B: **Which is manifest in our love for each other.**

CIRCLE-SHARED CROSS

This is a lovely way to greet a new member into a group.

1. The Shared Cross is performed by two people (see figure A.5a, page 186). When it is done, one of the people steps away toward the next one in the circle.

2. As the two people part, the sphere of light which surrounds them divides so that each remains in the sphere of light, the two spheres connected by a "cord" of light (see figure A.5b, page 186).

3. The Shared Cross is performed with the next person in circle. During this part of the ritual, when the sphere of light is formed in the center of the cross, it is even more brilliant than the light already there, and when the sphere is expanded, it is brighter still. This added brilliance extends to the original sphere as well.

4. As the person who is circling steps away from the second person, the sphere again divides (see figure A.5c, page 186).

5. This continues around the circle with the light becoming more and more brilliant as the energies of each person are added to it.

6. When the circle is completed, the circling person joins hands with the first, joining their spheres, then separating to form the cord of light, making a complete circle of light, studded with brilliant spheres, like a necklace of the Goddess.

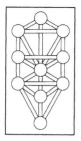

APPENDIX VI: RITUALS

HERE ARE TWO RITUALS with Qabalistic symbolism that are appropriate for use in Wicca. One is a self-dedication for someone wishing to begin serious work on a path of spiritual growth. The other is for use in a group with members who are having trouble.

DEDICATION TO THE JOURNEY

You will need for this ritual:

> A representation of the Tree of Life;
> A stick of incense at the east;
> A candle at the south;
> A cup of water at the west;
> Leaves of a fragrant herb at the north.

You should be familiar with the English names of the spheres.

Cast your circle in a way with which you are comfortable. Basic circle castings can be found in many books.

Touch Kether on your Tree of Life, imagining that a sphere of light fills the sphere drawn there. Say:

I seek the Crown—

Move your finger to Chokmah, seeing a line of light follow
your finger, and filling the sphere with light.

of Wisdom

Move your finger to Binah.

and understanding

Move to Chesed.

That Mercy

Move to Geburah.

and Might

Move to Tifareth.

In balance may bring Beauty

Move to Netzach.

Victory

Move to Hod.

and Glory

Move to Yesod.

Find their Foundation

Move to Malkuth.

In the Kingdom.

Now say,

So did my soul travel from Nothing to physical being. So does it long to return to its Source.

If you are not already there, go to the east of your ritual space.

Yet I know that to return as I am would be to return empty-handed, bringing nothing. I must learn the lessons of Air . . .

Light the incense and pass your hands through the smoke. Go to the south and say,

of Fire,

Light your candle and pass your hands through the flame. Go to the west and say,

of Water,

Dip your hands in the water. Go to the North and say,

and of Earth.

Rub your hands with the herb. Return to your beginning place.

To the learning of these lessons do I dedicate my life, my love, my Self.

Touch the sphere of Binah, and say,

Mother of all, hold me in your arms, and comfort me. Help me learn and grow.

Touch the sphere of Chokmah, saying,

Father of All, hold me in your arms, help me to be strong.

Touch the sphere of Chesed, saying:

Rulers of all, help me expand my spirit.

Touch the sphere of Geburah, saying:

Warriors, judges, give me courage. Help me to rid myself of that which is an obstacle on my journey.

Touch the sphere of Tifareth, saying;

Sacred children, I am but a child in spirit. Let us grow together. Lord and Ladies of the Sun, shine your warmth on me, and give me light to see. Sacrificed Gods, teach me thy Mysteries. Those who give illumination, bring your light to my soul.

Touch the sphere of Netzach, saying:

Lord and Ladies who are Love, help me to know all its faces, to give love and to receive it.

Touch the sphere of Hod, saying:

Lord and Ladies who teach, my mind and spirit are open to your lessons.

Touch the sphere of Yesod, saying:

Lord and Ladies of the Moon, reveal that which is hidden, and give me guidance in the darkness.

Touch the sphere of Malkuth, saying:

Lord and Ladies of growing things, give me health and fertility, that I may move forward.

Either prick your finger to obtain a drop of blood, or touch your finger to your tongue, and place the liquid on the sphere of Malkuth.

This, which contains all that I am, signifies my first step on my journey home. May the Gods and Goddesses all bless me.

Pause a moment, still touching the sphere, then say:

The Kingdom

Move your finger to Yesod, saying:

Finds its Foundation

Move to Hod and say,

In Splendor

Move to Netzach.

and Victory.

Move to Tifareth.

Beauty is the balance

Move to Geburah.

of Might

Move to Chesed.

and Mercy.

Move to Binah.

Understanding

Move to Chokmah.

and Wisdom

Move to Kether.

Will lead me to the Crown.

Look heavenward, and with all your heart, say:

So mote it be.

Sit and spend some time in contemplation of what you have done. When you are ready, close your circle.

THE RITE OF MENDING LOVE

This ritual is to be used when the dissension between two members of a circle is such that the circle is threatened. It must, obviously, be entered into freely by the two people involved. It must also be preceded by some serious work by the two involved in solving the problems that have existed between them, and the work must continue after the ritual has taken place.

While most of the ritual is performed by the two quarreling members, presided over by the High Priest or High Priestess, the other members of the circle should add their energies to each step.

It must be kept in mind by all, especially the two quarreling members, that during the lighting of the orange, green, and yellow candles, each speaks for both. When one says "Let unreasoning anger be blown away," they are *both* saying it.

Where the Deity Names used are Isis and Osiris, you may use the names normally used by your coven, or simply "Lady" and "Lord."

Where the instructions read "HP/S," it is left to your discretion whether the High Priestess or High Priest speaks, or if the words are shared by both.

A central altar should be set up following figure A.6 (page 196), with four candles at each quadrant: the three nearest the edge symbolizing the spheres of Hod, Tifareth, and Netzach.

The single candle placed nearer the center represents the element of that quadrant. My tradition uses yellow for Air, red for Fire, blue for Water, and green for Earth. You should, of course, follow the attributions of your own tradition if they differ.

If, as is the case with Air and Earth in my tradition, some elemental colors match the Qabalistic colors, you should use different shades of that color. For example, use a bright emerald for Netzach and a forest green for Earth.

There should also be two violet candles kept nearby, preferably the 7-day candles in glass. One of these should be provided by each of the quarreling members, and should be decorated in some way in symbols that have meaning to those who decorated them. The glass containers could be painted with designs. Another method is to use the "pullout" style—the candle will come out of the glass container and can itself be painted. Alternatively, designs can be carved into the wax. If you wish, honey can then be painted into the design and colored glitter applied to it.

You'll also need some healing oil, and a work knife. The method of circle-casting is left to you.

Circle is cast

High Priestess: **Hail, Isis, Mother of us all. We do ask your help in this our time of need. Two of your children have come to resolve their differences with your help. They come before you to ask your guidance in their trouble, knowing that by their dissension they weaken not only themselves, but the circle as well.**

High Priest: **Hail, Osiris, Father of us all. We have need of help and we do call upon you. Your aid is asked in resolving the**

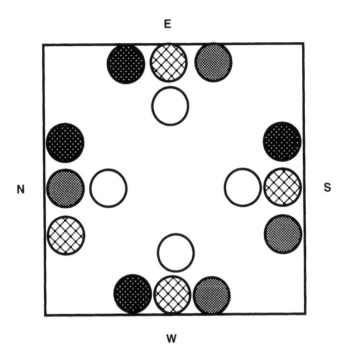

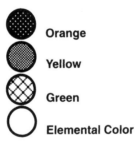

Figure A.6.   Altar Arrangement.

problems between two of your children, for they know that
their conflict hurts not only themselves, but the rest of us.

The two quarreling members (hereafter referred to as Quarreling Member 1 and Quarreling Member 2) come forward. The
High Priest and High Priestess face them.

High Priest or Priestess: **An incomplete circle is not a circle.
Without fellowship, without love among all its sisters and
brothers, this circle cannot be complete. Therefore, let us banish all anger, all argument between you, with the help of our
Gods.**

Quarreling Member 1: **Isis, my Mother, Osiris, my Father, I do
ask your help in banishing the dissension between my
brother/sister _____ and myself.**

Quarreling Member 2: **Isis, my Mother, Osiris, my Father, I do
ask your help in sending away the conflicts between my
brother/sister _____ and myself.**

All four go to the center altar, at the east side, facing west.

High Priest or Priestess: **Mercury, Hermes, Tehuti, all ye Gods
of Hod, Gods of Reason and Communication, hear me. Let
your powers of logic and reason enter these children of the God
and Goddess, circle them that they may use these powers in
their dealings with each other.**

Quarreling Member 1 takes up the orange candle. At each quadrant, Quarreling Member 1 lights the candle from the proper
elemental candle, speaks, then hands the candle to Quarreling
Member 2 who touches the candle again to the elemental candle, speaks, and replaces the candle on the altar.

Quarreling Member 1: **Let unreasoning anger be blown away;**

Quarreling Member 2: **And replaced with sensibility and logic.**

To the South

Quarreling Member 1: **Let angry words without meaning burn away;**

Quarreling Member 2: **And be replaced with the light of true communication.**

To the West

Quarreling Member 1: **Let misunderstandings be washed from memory;**

Quarreling Member 2: **And leave only those moments of true sharing.**

To the North

Quarreling Member 1: **Let the wall we have built between us crumble;**

Quarreling Member 2: **And become a smooth road we may walk together.**

Return to the East.

High Priest or Priestess: **Venus, Aphrodite, Rhiannon, Goddesses of Netzach, Goddesses of Love in all forms, hear me. Let your powers of love, of caring, of joy, enter these children of the God and Goddess, circle them that they may use these powers in their dealings with each other.**

Quarreling Member 1 takes up the green candle and lights it, saying:

Quarreling Member 1: **Let the air between us contain only love;**

Quarreling Member 2: **And the winds of change bring a stronger friendship.**

To the South

Quarreling Member 1: **Let the powers of Fire bring warmth to our relationship;**

Quarreling Member 2: **And the light of love banish the darkness of anger.**

To the West

Quarreling Member 1: **Let the powers of Water clean our friendship of its past harmful influences;**

Quarreling Member 2: **And heal the wounds we've given each other.**

To the North

Quarreling Member 1: **Let the powers of Earth strengthen our love for each other;**

Quarreling Member 2: **That we may strengthen each other with that love.**

Return to the East.

High Priest or Priestess: **Gods of Tifareth, Gods of Beauty and Harmony, hear me. Let your powers of balance, of rebirth, enter these children of the God and Goddess, circle them that they may use these powers in dealing with each other.**

Quarreling Member 1 takes the up yellow candle.

Quarreling Member 1: **The winds have blown away the imbalancing forces against us.**

Quarreling Member 2: **Let us share the cool and pleasant breezes.**

To the South

Quarreling Member 1: **The fires have burned away our anger.**

Quarreling Member 2: **Let us share the warmth and light of the Moon.**

To the West

Quarreling Member 1: **The rains have washed away the sorrows we've given each other.**

Quarreling Member 2: **Let us share the soothing sounds of the waves.**

To the North

Quarreling Member 1: **We have planted the seeds of true friendship in the fertile earth.**

Quarreling Member 2: **Let us share the work of tending them, and the pleasure in their growing.**

The two return to the East, take up the purple candles. Each pours healing oil onto the candle.

When the candles are prepared, they are lighted. QM1 presents a candle to the God and Goddess, asking a blessing, then turns to QM2 holding out the candle. QM2 places hands on the candle and they both hold it as QM2 speaks.

Quarreling Member 1: **The candle in the color of Spirit, is a symbol of my love for the Gods, and for you. As it burns, let it burn away those astral beings that represent anything other than friendship and love between us. As this candle grows smaller, so does any chance of misunderstanding. As the space above the candle grows larger, so does the strength of the bond between us. Will you accept this candle and its meanings, giving in return your forgiveness for my thoughtlessness and foolishness?**

Quarreling Member 2 responds. The candle is placed on altar. Quarreling Member 2 takes up the other purple candle, presents it for a blessing, then presents it to Quarreling Member 1, saying:

Quarreling Member 2: **This candle is in a color that blends Might and Mercy, and also signifies the sphere beyond the physical. As it burns, let it light our way to a greater understanding of each other. As the candle becomes smaller, so will the space between us. As the space above it grows larger, let our love for each other grow. Will you accept this candle and its meanings, giving in return your forgiveness for any pain I may have caused you?**

Quarreling Member 1 responds. The candle is placed on the altar. Quarreling Member 1 and Quarreling Member 2 turn to each other, join hands and perform the Alternate Shared Cross. They should stand together as long as they feel it necessary. At this point, they may add anything they feel appropriate, such as an exchange of gifts, or whatever words come to mind. They then return to their original places in the circle.

High Priest or Priestess: **Once again we are a complete circle.**

Group joins hands.

High Priest or Priestess: **Once again the energies pass from one to the other, ever-growing in strength and skill. We are an un-broken chain, each link complete within itself, and each link joined to the next. Our circle is whole again. Let us rejoice in our hearts for ourselves and for our brother/sister _____ and our brother/sister _____.**

Close the circle.

RECOMMENDED READING

The following books are only a few of those available. Others will be found in the bibliography. This list has not changed from the first edition of this book, not because other good books haven't been published since, but because I have not found any books that would replace those listed here. If they have gone out of print, they are worth searching for.

The books on this list will give you as complete an understanding of the mystical Qabala as any teaching method can. Qabala, more than any other subject, is best learned through study and meditation. Just as teachers cannot teach you the mysteries, no book, however excellent, can teach you Qabala, but can only lead you toward an understanding of its Mysteries. The personal work you do, the amount of effort you are willing to put forth, control the amount you gain.

These authors do not always agree with each other, nor will you agree with every one of them (nor do I). All the better, because it will teach you that you must make up your own mind. It will also teach you that nothing any of these excellent authors say should be carved in stone. Read these books, think about what they've said, and choose what works for you. (Are you getting tired of hearing that?)

Don't let any comments made by these authors keep you from learning from them. They each have much to share with you, if you are open to receiving it. Some of the comments reflect prejudices against homosexuals, and some against witches. (One of them defended his comments on the subject by reminding me that his book was written before information was widely available. He promises not to do it any more.) In spite of the Qabala's recognition of the Goddess, many of the books are extremely God-oriented. Don't be foolish. These authors are sharing years of experience and work with you. Let them share it.

The Mystical Qabalah by Dion Fortune: One of the best books to be found. It will give you superb basic knowledge to work with.

Ladder of Lights by W. G. Gray: Its arrangement and presentation of the material is very different from most books on Qabala. Gray concentrates on the Four Worlds of each sphere and this approach is of immeasurable value in developing your understanding of them.

A Practical Guide to Qabalistic Symbolism by Gareth Knight: I have a two-volume set, but I believe this has since been published in one volume. This book contains enough suggestions or meditations to keep you busy for years. The rest of the information is just as helpful. Gareth Knight is a Christian Qabalist, and many of his references are from the Christian mythos. This can be helpful to those with a Christian background, but distracting to those without. It would be a shame to miss the information in this book because you lack tolerance of another faith.

Occult Psychology by A. LaDage: With or without a psychological background, you will gain a lot from this interface of Qabala with Jungian psychology.

An Introduction to the Mystical Qabala by Alan Richardson: This little book is especially helpful in applying Qabala to your magical work.

The Sword And The Serpent by Denning and Phillips: This book is the result of study and experience by a modern magical lodge and offers yet another point of view. For example, the authors present alternate color scales you might prefer to the "traditional" one. This volume is one in a series called *The Magical Philosophy*.

The Tree of Life by Israel Regardie: Along with information on the Qabala, this will introduce you to other aspects of ceremonial magic and its ideologies that you may find useful.

If you wish to continue to look for more information about the paths between the spheres, the following books will be helpful:

Practical Guide to Qabalistic Symbolism, Volume 2 by Gareth Knight: The information to be gained by working each path is included here, as well as various correspondences. Both volumes of this work will appeal to those of you who are artists, because they contain descriptions that cry to be painted.

The Living Tree by W. G. Gray: Mr. Gray, as always, chooses his own individual way of expressing himself, and his own very unusual attributions to the paths. It is a very interesting book.

The Witches Tarot by Ellen Cannon Reed: This explores the paths in much the same way as I've explored the spheres.

Most of the books on this list have been with me since I first began to study Qabala, and I've read each of them many times. When I began to teach Qabala, I re-read all of them. During the preparation of a lecture on the subject, I read them yet again. Each time certain phrases leaped to my eye, certain sentences and paragraphs were especially meaningful. The amazing thing was that they were never the same phrases or paragraphs. The "purple patches" were, each time, those which related to my own status at each reading: student, teacher, lecturer, writer.

Even in written form, Qabala is wondrous!

BIBLIOGRAPHY

Ashcroft-Nowicki, Dolores. *The Shining Paths: An Experience in Vision of the 12 Paths of the Tree of Life.* Wellingborough, England: Aquarian Press. 1983.

Bhagavad Gita As It Is. Swami Prabhubada, trans. New York: Bhaktivedanta Book Trust.

Butler, W. E., *Magic and the Qabala.* London: Aquarian Press, 1964.

Chaucer, Geoffrey. *The Portable Chaucer,* Theodore Morrison, ed. New York: Viking Press, 1975.

Crowley, Aleister. *777 and other Qabalistic Writings.* York Beach, ME: Samuel Weiser, 1986.

Denning, Melitta, and Osborne Phillips. *Sword and the Serpent.* St. Paul, MN: Llewellyn, 1975.

Donavon, Frank. *Never on a Broomstick.* Harrisburg, PA: Stackpole Books, 1971.

Douglas, Lloyd C. *Green Light.* New York: Grosset & Dunlap, 1935.

Einstein, Albert. *What I Believe.* New York: Crossroads, 1984.

Fortune, Dion. *The Mystical Qabalah.* York Beach, ME: Samuel Weiser, 1984.

Frank, Adolph. *The Kabbalah.* Secaucus, NJ: University Books, 1967.

Frazer, Sir James. *The Golden Bough.* New York: McMillan, 1974.

Gibran, Kahlil. *The Prophet.* New York: Alfred A. Knopf, 1923.

Grahame, Kenneth. *The Wind in the Willows.* New York: Tor Books, 1989.

Grant, Joan. *Winged Pharoah.* Columbus, OH: Ariel Press, 1985.

Graves, Robert. *The White Goddess.* Winchester, MA: Faber & Faber, 1947.

Gray, William G. *Ladder of Lights*. York Beach, ME: Samuel Weiser, 1993.

———. *The Living Tree*. Cheltenham, England: Helios Books, 1958.

Hall, Manly P. *Cabalistic Keys to the Lord's Prayer*. Los Angeles: Philosophical Research Society, 1964.

Hawkridge, Emma. *The Wisdom Tree*. Boston: Houghton Mifflin, 1945.

Jung, C. G. *Contributions to Analytical Psychology*. 1928.

Knight, Gareth. *Practical Guide to Qabalistic Symbolism*. York Beach, ME: Samuel Weiser, 1978.

Kraig, Donald Michael. *Modern Magic*. St. Paul, MN: Llewellyn, 1988.

Kunitz, Stanley. "The Flight of Apollo" in *The Poems of Stanley Kunitz 1928–1978*. Boston: Little, Brown, 1979.

LaDage, Alta. *Occult Psychology*. St. Paul, MN: Llewellyn, 1987.

Levi, Eliphas. *The Book of Splendors*. York Beach, ME: Samuel Weiser, 1973.

Low, Collin. *Note on Kaballah*. http://www/digital-brilliance.com/kab/nok/index.html.

Moody, Raymond. *Life after Life*. New York: Bantam, 1976.

Parker, Dorothy. *The Poems & Short Stories of Dorothy Parker*. New York: Random House, 1994.

Ponce, Charles. *Kabbalah*. Wheaton, IL: Theosophical Publishing House, 1978.

Reed, Ellen Cannon. *The Witches Tarot*. St. Paul, MN: Llewellyn, 1989.

Regardie, Israel. *Art of True Healing*. Cheltenham, England: Helios, 1974.

———. *The Complete Golden Dawn System of Magic*. Phoenix: New Falcon, 1984.

———. *Garden of Pomegranates*. St. Paul, MN: Llewellyn, 1974.

———. *Golden Dawn*. St. Paul, MN: Llewellyn, 1982.

———. *Middle Pillar*. St. Paul, MN: Llewellyn, 1970.

———. *The Tree of Life*. York Beach, ME: Samuel Weiser, 1983.

Richardson, Alan. *Introduction to the Mystical Qabala.* New York: Samuel Weiser, 1974.

Santayana, George. *The Sense of Beauty.* New York: Dover, 1896.

Schaya, L. *Universal Meaning of the Kabbalah.* Secaucus, NJ: University Books, 1971.

Seven Pupils of E. G. *Mysteries of the Qabala.* Chicago: Yogi Publications Society, 1922.

Sinclair, David. *Drum and Candle.* Garden City, NY: Doubleday, 1971.

Twain, Mark. *Roughing it.* New York: NAL/Dutton, 1962.

Von Rosenroth, Aesch. *Mexareph.* New York: Occult Research Press, n.d.

Westcott, W. Wynn. *Sepher Yetzirah.* New York: Samuel Weiser, 1975.

INDEX

212   INDEX